HOW TO BE AN INDUSTRY A-PLAYER

YOUNG
GUN

THE A-Z GUIDE FOR AMBITIOUS CONSTRUCTORS TO STAND OUT AND SUCCEED

**2-TIME
BESTSELLING AUTHOR**

ELINOR
MOSHE

KMD
BOOKS

First published in Australia in 2022
by KMD Books
Waikiki, WA 6169

Cover design by Dylan Ingram

Edited by Chelsea Wilcox

Typeset in Adobe Garamond Pro 12.5/18pt

A catalogue record for this
work is available from the
NATIONAL
LIBRARY National Library of Australia
OF AUSTRALIA

National Library of Australia Catalogue-in-Publication data:

Young Gun/Elinor Moshe

ISBN:
978-0-6454374-4-7
(Hardback)

ISBN:
978-0-6454374-8-5
(Paperback)

ISBN:
978-0-6454374-9-2
(Ebook)

To those with hunger in their stomach, vision in their mind, and fire in their heart.

As always, to Mum and Dad, Ron and Caroline.

CONTENTS

INTRODUCTION

It's Sunday night. Tomorrow's the day. The one that you have been longing and hoping for. The one that you dreamt about all those nights dragging yourself through university, wondering what it's all for. Alas, now the sense of anticipation teamed with excitement and nervousness sweeps over you. You're finally starting your professional career in construction. The days of rejection emails and false hopes of interviews are over. No more opening your inbox and immediately scanning the emails for the word 'unfortunately', as you stared down the barrel of rejection after rejection. No more answering and quelling your parents'concerns as to what you are planning to do with your life, and when will you start work. I am sure this sounds familiar to you.

Yet here we are. You're starting in approximately twelve hours. You're possibly not used to waking up early anymore, given the anarchy that has ruled your schedule between part-time work and university deadlines. Now, your clothes are ready to go, you just sit and wait. And the questions start flooding your mind …

What should I do on my first day?

What do I need to bring?

What if they don't like me and think they made a mistake hiring me?

What if they find out I don't know anything?

What if I don't know what to do and ask a silly question?

How will I learn all that I need to?

What if I don't do a great job?

What if, what if, what if …

There's a whole host of questions that race through your mind as you stand on the precipice of the next chapter of your life. First, I want to congratulate you on arriving at this point in your destination. Through the mentoring that I do with my clients, and having gone through the turbulence myself, I'm well acquainted with the journey leading up to you getting that one yes in a barrel of noes. You can be proud of your achievements to date, but what you've just experienced is not the most challenging part of your career. The real work is about to begin. Your career, after all, is anywhere between three to five decades long. The most dangerous part is actually when you get employment, as it can start to fuel an over-reliance on the employer for your development, and when the zest for personal and professional development stops for a significant period of time. Whilst many think they're moving forward, it starts the slow regression backwards.

Except, you're not going to front the start of your career alone. You're going to be fully armed going in. Above the whole host of questions that race through your mind, there's also a whole host of considerations that you don't know that you don't know when standing at the outset of your professional career. And that's why I had to write this book for you. To be your guidance, inspiration and direction to fuel your ambition and highlight you as the young gun that you really are. So that your new employers can look at you in due time and say that you are the best decision that they've made for the company. So that you can also get the best experience out of the formative days of your career instead of falling into the trap of mediocre professional practices. And so that you are a cut above the rest in every opportunity that you meet as you build the foundations to your career. The corporate world is filled with mediocre mindsets and skillsets and that's not what the construction industry needs moving forward. It needs brilliant executives, entrepreneurs and leaders who are pining for the best of the best in the industry to be on their team. Except that talent pool is shrinking at an alarming rate. We need the young guns to truly stand out and succeed, to raise the standard of the collective and truly make the industry an incredible one to be in for the long haul. Doesn't that sound like a future worth constructing?

Of great importance then: Who is a young gun?

A young gun is someone who (including but not limited to):

- Is driven by a burning desire and passion for the construction industry.
- Is driven by their high standards set for themselves and strives for and adheres to excellence as the minimum

standard in everything they do.

- Is a maximalist in the sense that they are seeking more in every arena of their life.
- Places value on industry contribution and betterment.
- Goes over and above all expectations and is a true high performer.
- Is a non-conformist and doesn't seek to follow the herd.
- Invests in their mindset and skillset by not relying on their employer for growth and development opportunities.
- Plays the long-term game by delaying gratification and takes calculated risks to progress in their career.
- Has a bold, large, captivating vision for their lives and the industry.

The unique alchemy and composition of the inputs that make up a young gun and the categories which you can expect the A-Z to fall under is represented in The Ambitious Young Gun Framework. The combination of high-performance principles of success, high standard professional practices and unconventional career intelligence to be the guide for excellence in achievement is what you can expect to learn from this book. To be a young gun is pillared on these three spheres to ensure a holistic approach to growth and development is provided, from the inside out. Otherwise, most people just aim for a tactical or degree-based approach to success, which only yields further conventional outcomes. Society as a whole doesn't need more successful people – society needs successful people who will raise the modus operandi around them and contribute to creating more successful people who can do the same.

Taking the conventional and
predictable career route

High
performance
principles of
success

High standard
professional
practices

Missing out on opportunity to
be a stand out success

Not maximising value
to others

Unconventional
career intelligence
for excellence in
achievememt

The sweet spot -
The Young Gun

The Ambitious Young Gun Framework ™

I will provide you with all the insights, advice and considerations that I have garnered in my eight years of working in commercial construction, to allow you to bypass the time it takes to learn the the nuances of the game. Considerably throughout my own journey, especially in the formative years, I would frequently find myself saying, 'Well I wish someone told me that earlier.' That 'someone' is this book. Your time to shine is now. Don't you want to bring your A-game? This book is your guide and roadmap as you enter the construction industry, giving you the personal and professional principles and practices that make up the A-players of the industry. This is what they do and don't do, so you can follow suit and enter a league of champions.

If you are reading this thinking, *There's no chance this could be me,* that is a self-imposed limitation upon your own mindset. Whilst some characteristics are fixed within people, some are developable, and that is what this book sets out to guide you on. I wrote this book for the exemplary leaders and industry titans who are being formed and moulded *today* that are going to be household names in ten years, or less, from now. Of course, this potential lies in everyone. Except there was a striking experience which, in retrospect, served as the seed for this book. When I worked in corporate, I'd finished working on a construction site, and for the first time in five years, was heading back into head office to commence project administration work for a recently awarded project. Personally, I was relieved at the thought of a hygienic environment where I didn't have to fear everything I touched being covered in dust and was graced with a proper kitchen. As I walked to and from my desk a few times during the day, I noticed the cadets glued to their screens, in silence. I certainly understand their hesitation as cadets to not speak to seniors, but to generally be muted and static day in and out didn't make sense. I reflected to the start of my career, even when I worked in an office in the early years it wasn't like that. I may not have had the confidence I possess today, but I wasn't glued to my screen and certainly not a static mute. I thought about it from their perspective – was this the dream that these young con-struction graduates held for themselves? Or did they not know what to do, that would be couth or accepted? A mixture of both. I saw the same in my clients who'd entered industry. They lacked the guidelines, the playbook of best practice at their stage. There are more than enough standards and codes for building construc-tion, but what about the people behind the projects?

There are those who will continue to be mute and glued to their screen, but there are those who you can tell from the outset are going to be the next industry leaders, the next entrepreneurs, the next Thought Leaders. They're fierce, they're determined, they're hungry. They're not cut from the same fabric as everyone else. They're ambitious and driven to the core, and simply want more in every sense of their career. They're not easily satisfied, and they are not mediocre by any measure – they're simply excellent in their roles and carry themselves with high integrity and earn respect.

There are further considerations that a young gun starting off needs to consider from a broader, career-intelligence perspective, such as the importance and value of mentoring, setting goals, having a vision and the like. Albeit important factors to the inner development of a young gun, this has been covered in my first book, *Constructing Your Career,* and purposely omitted from this one. A young gun is also the one set for future leadership positions, and as much as L for Leadership would have been fitting, I've also extensively covered leadership in my second book, *Leadership in Construction.* I would encourage these resources as complimentary to your development. If you are well into your corporate career and choose to read this, then you can certainly up your game all the same, as A-Z is just as relevant.

At the end of each section, you will find a section titled Trigger Questions and Young Gun Bullets. The Trigger Questions are to encourage you to think critically about the letter you have just read about and start considering the application and importance of it for your career. The questions are designed to take you into considered reflection, so I encourage you to not take the first surface-level answer you generate. Learn to sit with the questions and dig deeper within yourself. Young Gun Bullets are actionable steps that will allow you to practically demonstrate the content discussed. Each bullet is there to fill your magazine to load your (metaphorical) gun with. So, you are always ready to lock and load and be ready to go. The bullets vary over timeframes, and to get the best results, tweak and monitor the process and progress. However, it's up to you to take the ideas learnt within the book and translate them to your reality. The transformation that you are looking for is always in the execution.

So, let's get you off the starting line with a roaring start, to stand out and demonstrate what a brilliant and remarkable young gun you really are. You won't need to worry about doing a great job if you follow this guide with concision and consistency. Success can be yours in volumes yet to be imagined.

Ready?

Aim, load and fire!

A

AMBITION

ĂM-BĬSH′əN

AN EAGER OR STRONG DESIRE

TO ACHIEVE SOMETHING

---

*'At the age of six, I wanted to be a cook. At seven, I wanted
to be Napoleon. And my ambition has been growing steadily
ever since.' – Salvador Dali*

Did you notice on the cover that this book is for *ambitious* constructors? It's not for a constructor who is going to be satisfied doing the bare minimum (yet paradoxically hoping to receive the absolute maximum). It's not for constructors who are content with cruising by, taking a laid-back approach and simply hoping for the best. A young gun can only be a young gun if they possess ambition. To be ambitious is to desire constant progression, growth and more. Because of my level of ambition, I don't even attract the type of people to my world who haven't got any. They have no desire to work with me (well, no desire generally to work on anything other than their nine to five and that's only because they get paid for it). I'm a maximalist, whereas most people are content with the bare minimum. The people who come into my world are those with ambition. They desire more, even if they don't know what that is just yet. The fact that you are reading this book would suggest that you already have more ambition than most. There are unfortunately people in this world who still seek the benefit of reading a book without reading one. Ambition isn't a quality that you can teach someone to have, it's innate. And whilst it may seem common, it's surprisingly not. I highlight this quality and distinction to you first, so you can already start to see how much opportunity there is for your ambition and how uniquely positioned you already are. Whilst it may seem that the industry is flooded with young guns, it's not. The Industry Target shows that the smallest professional share is made up of young guns. It's not the pathway most commonly taken at all.

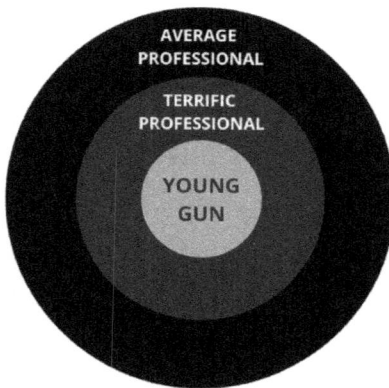

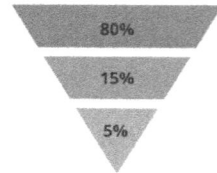

Where to aim your gun - The Industry Target ™

Market share composition of each type of professional

YOUNG GUN PRINCIPLE

Young guns are ambitious and do not seek to quell it or hide it but have it proudly on display. Ambition is the key winning trait of future leaders and entrepreneurs in the industry, which is why you must be in the constant pursuit of your goals and ambitions.

Ambitious people desire more, as they are constantly in the pursuit of achievement. We have high achievement orientation, which means we place high priority on accomplishment and success. This isn't purely reflective of ambitions to do with the material world. We set high goals for ourselves and then set out to achieve them, and in the process being willing to do what others won't, so as also to have what others won't. It also means that we are constantly dissatisfied with our present situation and are always on the lookout for what we can do next. Contrary to what society and cultural norms say, there is nothing wrong with this. If it wasn't for people who are driven to achieve, challenge norms and do more, then there would be no value production, innovation or raised standards of living. Having high achievement orientation is a mindset that is continually focused on betterment, driving excellent performance (personally and in those around you) and running to challenges, not away from them. Ambitious people are hungry for success (per their own definition) and do not rest or back down until they have that sense of accomplishment. Accomplishment is also addictive, as we get hooked on the pursuit and the journey, and the growth that comes with progress, rather than the destination itself. Which is why you see the ambitious people constantly moving and forging new territory ahead. Society has made ambition out to be a dirty word, yet there is nothing wrong with having ambition. I think ambition is a beautiful thing, for the lack of it results in mediocrity – people being satisfied with average lives and heading down paths that are self-serving – is of no benefit to anyone around them. I mention this all to you so you nurture your ambitious streak. Plus, only those who have less ambition than you will criticise you.

> 'Without ambition one starts nothing. Without work one finishes nothing. The prize will not be sent to you. You have to win it.'
> – Ralph Waldo Emerson

Ambition is a distinctive trait that impactful and successful leaders and entrepreneurs have. And that's why it was imperative for me to make this book out to the ambitious young guns, as you will be the face and backbone of the construction industry in the not-too-distant future. You will be the CEOs, Thought Leaders and founders of the future, and the earlier that you get into the standard of excellence instead of mediocrity, the better for everyone involved. For an individual to achieve such career heights takes hunger, takes ambition. You can't tell a person who is locked into their comfort zone – that has no desire to take any risks or temporarily sacrifice pleasure in the pursuit of an ambition to aspire to greatness – to demand more from themselves. People are not truly ambitious unless they are willing to make sacrifices in the pursuit of their ambition. However, for most, it's not even in their line of sight or train of thought. But those with ambition already have their heart and mind set to great heights, and this is what's required of future leaders and future entrepreneurs. If leaders and entrepreneurs aren't focused on constructing tomorrow and thinking about what could be next, then assuredly no-one else is. That's why adding fuel to the flames of ambition is imperative to a young gun today. Otherwise, who will lead tomorrow? There's only a lot of competition in the lower to mid tiers of corporations. The competition slims down as you go up because of what it truly takes to become exceptional.

Ambitious people also prefer aligning themselves with other ambitious people, and this is a trait that, time and time again from conversations with industry leaders, is confirmed is hard to find. Ambitious people are rare, and I dare say, getting rarer with the comforts of the modern world. Think about it. A young gun who has success for one or two years can quickly be on a near six-figure salary. This is just about enough for a new car, all living expenses covered, dinners out and other small luxuries and an annual holiday. Doesn't that sound great to most? It sure does, because that's all they have to show for their efforts. Where is the inspiration and motivation then to leave the comfort zone and take on an ambitious undertaking? It's rare, which is why you see most people opt for a pure corporate career rather than any other modality of having a career. When you demonstrate your ambition and zest, people of the same calibre will notice this within you, which can provide incredible pathways. I know this for a fact, as it's what afforded me opportunities in two years that people can only dream of in twenty. Your ambition is your key on the success highway. Alternatively, you can take the slow lane or the bus. Ambition can't be taught, it's inherent in an individual or not, and this rare attribute will be seen far and wide in the industry should you respectfully and credibly have it on display. The people in positions of influence today are looking for it.

YOUNG GUN PRINCIPLE

The task of an ambitious young gun is never accomplished, and they must never be suspended in motion by temporary defeat or resistance. The success is in the consistent application of effort against all odds.

In *The Republic,* a Socratic dialogue authored by Plato, he pens that, 'Being devoid of ambition, good men shun politics, leaving us to be ruled by bad men and their ambitions.' Remember that your ambition is a constructive force, not a destructive force. And if your good ambition isn't used for the greater good, then what is the alternative? To this day, people still speak of ambition after Aristotle as 'healthy ambition', 'unhealthy ambition' and 'lack of ambition'. Healthy ambition can be understood as the measured striving for achievement or distinction, and unhealthy ambition as the immoderate or disordered striving for such. Healthy ambition is individually enabling and socially constructive, while unhealthy ambition is inhibiting, destructive and more akin to greed. Lack of ambition is a regression as everything around you moves at increasingly faster speeds and is non-existent.

And finally, being ambitious is also akin to being competitive. If a person is truly wired for progress, then they are inherently competitive. I want to win, I want to see you win and you should want to see yourself win. Ambitious people have this innate need to win, and there is nothing wrong with that, on the proviso it's done within all moral and ethical bounds. You will find people who are truly hungry for success are deeply disappointed in getting a mere participation award– they want to win. The distinction I will make is that you should always only be in competition with yourself. The competition is only to be a better version than you were this time last year. If you can still recognise yourself from one year ago, you haven't changed. Two years, and you have a fixed mindset not a growth mindset. Ambitious people are competitive, but it's the drive to constantly level up which is addictive. It's your duty to be better in every aspect of your life as time progresses, otherwise, what are you really doing with yourself?

Ambition is the requisite to standing out and succeeding. Ambition and achievement may be my first language, but I want it to be yours too.

TRIGGER QUESTIONS

1. Do you think you are truly ambitious in nature? And how ambitious are you?
2. What are the key motivators behind your ambition?
3. How have you expressed your ambition in the past?
4. Is your ambition self-serving or here to serve others?
5. Do you quell or express your ambitions openly?
6. How do you think high achievers think differently to those who are driven by mediocrity?

YOUNG GUN BULLETS

- Set three ambitious goals that you have never achieved for the next twelve months.
- Say yes to three upcoming new experiences that you would have previously rejected. For example, an opportunity to join a committee or undertake a mentoring program.
- Give yourself a score out of ten for each aspect of your life: career, health, financials, relationships, spirituality and contribution/community. Then score where you would like the figure to be. Come up with one goal to achieve per quarter to enable you to raise the score of each house. This is to enable you to learn to compete with yourself and focus on your own improvement by finding new ways to challenge yourself.

B

BRAND

BRĂND

A TRADEMARK OR DISTINCTIVE NAME IDENTIFYING

A PRODUCT, SERVICE OR ORGANISATION

'It's important to build a personal brand because it's the only thing you're going to have. Your reputation online, and in the new business world is pretty much the game, so you've got to be a good person. You can't hide anything, and more importantly, you've got to be out there at some level.' – Gary Vaynerchuk

What do you think will create the greatest degree of separation between you and the young gun sitting next to you?

Do you plan to compete with the next person on experience, skills and qualifications alone? If that's the case, you may say you have two degrees, the next person has three. So you go and get another one, only to find out the new person has four. Where do you draw the line?

And why do people who stand out get more exclusive opportunities than those who fit in?

The professional world is sleeping and dormant to the opportunities that come with having a personal brand. It's not that professionals don't have a personal brand, it's just one that hasn't been constructed based on their person and ensures they get continuously misunderstood. I considered carefully whether B should be for branding, and not a professional practice. But in reflection over my own career, my personal brand is what created the greatest distinction and competitive edge, second only to my mindset to stand out and succeed. I have one of the most distinctive, congruent and authentic personal brands in the construction industry. There was a time in my career, pre-personal brand, where I was a dulled-down, meek, diminished version of myself. Then there is the time afterwards, where I am all of who I am, confident and bold and inhabit my prerogative of standing out. Your personal brand is a precise and delicate piece of construction that captures the essence of who you are and works to build rapport with others en masse. In a world full of sameness and watered-down versions of people, being all of who you are and encapsulating this in a brand is one of the most valuable aspects you can have for your career.

YOUNG GUN PRINCIPLE

Having a personal brand ensures your individuality
is captured and not lost. Developing an authentic,
congruent and magnetic personal brand will enable you
to attract exclusive career opportunities and be truly seen
for who you are.

When I first entered the industry, I saw that most people in corporate spoke a certain way, dressed in a similar manner, and by sheer nature of training, carried out work in a similar way. On a subconscious level, what a person then deduces is that to succeed, *I must fit in.* And like waves hitting a cliff shore, slowly but surely over time, if you don't hold onto your individuality it will erode. And you will look back and not be able to pinpoint the moment that you lost yourself. There wasn't one particular moment where you became just another face in the crowd, wearing the same corporate jacket and same chinos like everyone else. It didn't happen all at once, but it happened. And then you go to a few events, and you can only identify yourself based on your job title. It's a stretch of your dialogue to talk about anything but work anymore. You have lost yourself completely. I know because that's what happened to me. And I am fortunate and grateful to the end of time that I was mentored by Ron Malhotra who enabled me to find myself. If you lose yourself, you lose it all. I lost myself once, and I will never do that again. Why do I share this with you? If you are just another indistinctive face making up the masses, you will also get the same results as that of the masses. What are the general results of the masses? They earn an average of $75,000 per year, with 70-80% of them feeling stuck in unfulfilled jobs. They have no high-income skillset, and they are stuck in a scarcity and fear-based modality of living. However …

Those who have a personal brand – which is an expression of an individuality – first get to experience their own person and have this innate confidence that comes with knowing and representing all of who you are. Second, a personal brand starts adding to your authority, wherever you are in the corporate ladder, and gets you noticed. This is exactly what businesses do – they build a brand to attract clientele. What makes you think you're immune to this? Opportunity will go to those who are noticed because they have a higher degree of distinction. And people who are distinct are memorable. Third, a personal brand controls your name in the marketplace. This is not to say I am responsible for a person's perception of my brand – call it confidence, call it arrogance, either is none of my business. But I am wholly in control of my name, messaging and brand. Someone can make an informed decision whether they want to connect with me, do business with me or collaborate with me. I know very well that the calibre of collaborations and conversations I have been able to pull is because of my brand. My brand alone has unlocked doors that would normally take years to access via the conventional route, if at all. The benefits of having a personal brand vary per person and are exponential. I spent one year building it and get to spend forever capitalising and building on it. Someone can copy what I do, what I wear, how I speak, how I write and even the colours and fonts of my brand, but it'll never work, as it has nothing to do with them. Your brand is the one thing which no-one can ever take away from you. However, as you can see, most won't invest one year to building an asset with exponential returns. If you follow suit, you will find yourself drowning as the professional marketplace gets increasingly more competitive. If your strategy to win is the same strategy that others use not to lose, expect a long, hard, struggling road ahead.

'Branding demands commitment; commitment to continual reinvention; striking chords with people to stir their emotions; and commitment to imagination. It is easy to be cynical about such things, much harder to be successful.' – Sir Richard Branson

The real benefit of developing a personal brand is that it requires you to know your person, as I've previously mentioned. When you know who you are, you can also make beneficial decisions for yourself. This is important, because as you enter the industry, there will be all too many at the ready to give you unsolicited advice and direction. They will advise you to be more like this, less like that. My natural disposition is to be direct and confident, why would I tone it down? A person who doesn't have a clue who they are can't be telling you to be more or less of anything. This is how people get washed away. Manager A on project A tells you to be more straightforward in your communication, then Manager B tells you to be less direct and become a yes-person. Manager C then comes along and tells you to be blunt and harsh to everyone. It's no wonder people don't recognise themselves. They have outsourced their personal development to authority. The only thing you need to be more of is all of who you are. Consider yourself a painting. You are better off completing the painting yourself, than letting anyone who walks by add or take away something from the canvas. The first would result in a masterpiece, the second option, well, use your imagination for that one.

TRIGGER QUESTIONS

1. What benefits do you see for yourself generating an authentic and congruent personal brand?
2. Do you currently feel mostly understood or misunderstood? Why?
3. How well do you feel you know your person? Could you describe your person sans degrees, experiences and job titles in less than sixty seconds?
4. If you weren't in the room, are people saying what you want them to be saying about you?
5. Is it important to you to stand out from the crowd and express your individuality? Why/why not?
6. What opportunities would you like to come to you if you had a stand-out and recognisable personal brand?

YOUNG GUN BULLETS

- The first step to branding is to know your person. Make an inventory of all your unique features, attributes, personality traits, values and strengths that make you, *you.*
- Write a one-page brand vision and mission, considering the brand experience, what you want to be known for, what you want to accomplish with your brand, and the characteristics and traits that you want your brand to be perceived as.
- Identify the message that you want to convey with your brand. What does your brand communicate about you when

you're not around? If you were to generate content about your brand, what would it say?

*Developing an authentic, congruent and magnetic personal brand is a six-to-twelve-month personalised development process. These bullets are to get you to start preparing the groundwork for the foundations of your brand.

C

COMMUNICATION

KƏ-MYOO″NĬ-KĀ′SHƏN
THE EXCHANGE OF THOUGHTS, MESSAGES OR
INFORMATION, AS BY SPEECH, SIGNALS,
WRITING OR BEHAVIOUR

---

*'The single biggest problem in communication is the illusion
that it has taken place.'* – George Bernard Shaw

'Did you call them?'

'No, I sent them an email ...'

It's a generational thing, that young graduates these days have an aversion to talking on the phone and having real-time conversations. We can thank social media for that, where people have a lag in real-time communication and can refine their words before relaying it to someone else. It's like a safety net to quell the fear of possibly saying the wrong thing. There is a muscle in our mind that is responsible for our ability to have real-time conversations, and if you are hiding behind your screen (otherwise known as keyboard warriors) then that muscle is weakened by the day. The trepidation with picking up the phone comes from not knowing what to say. Prior to picking up the phone, you can jot down a few talking points or questions, but please, pick up the phone. The justification will be *it's easier to send an email* or *it's not that urgent,* but that is not the point. Not only do you become more highly skilled at having real-time conversations and talking through problems and solutions, but you are building rapport with the project stakeholder.

Naturally there are some things which do need to be put in writing, and that best practice of keeping accurate project records isn't dissolved. But for example, if you intend to cut down a contractor's claim, call them to let them know that's what they can expect. If you were calling and chasing a subcontractor for pricing and were actively involved with them during the tender period, call to let them know they have been unsuccessful. Subcontractors understand the nature of the game, and whilst some tenders will be harder missing out on than others, they will still respect and be able to price for you the next time round if you were fair and equitable during the process. But have the phone conversation with them. If you need to go through a quotation, get on the phone. Of course, having responses in emails gives you the time to digest information at your own pace, but the skill is in the conversation, not being a keyboard warrior. There is a time and place for emails, and there is a time and place for picking up the phone, or even having a face-to-face conversation. Do not shy away from the latter two, as your success moving forward is going to be heavily predicated on your ability to have it. You are taking the long and hard road of building your communication repertoire and capability by hiding behind the keyboard. At worst, if you get on the phone and it's starting to sound like a disaster, you can always say that you're new and will have to get back to them with the information or do more reconnaissance before you answer their question.

Talking on the phone is not the scariest thing in the world, but to young guns who've recently entered the industry, it is. Follow these steps in making professional phone calls to increase your confidence:

1. Prepare for the call by noting what information you need to convey or attain. You can jot down the key points you need to cover or questions to ask.

2. You can start with some banter, but don't feel the need to overdo the small talk. Don't overuse filler sentences or be apologetic about the call. Tell the person the intention of your call without using, 'I'm just calling you/hope I'm not bothering you.' After the small talk, just say, 'I'm calling in regard to ...'

3. As you are talking, take notes. The fear-inducing part for young guns on the phone typically stems from not knowing what to respond with or being unable to recall what was said. You would just take that question on notice and advise the person that you don't know (even if you don't know something, say 'I don't know' with confidence) and that you will get back to them with accurate information.

4. End the call by repeating any action items or what was

agreed, including any timelines for follow up. If needed, put the conversation in writing for posterity as to what was said, especially if it has cost, time or other project implications.

YOUNG GUN PRINCIPLE

Pick up the phone and make it your mission to not avoid real-time conversations. Communication is the skill that will unlock the most opportunities so be proactive in developing this.

Which, of course, brings me to email etiquette. Considering how much time is spent behind a screen dealing with stakeholders via email, who teaches a young gun how to write great emails? It's one of the aspects which seems a given, but most young guns aren't given the principles of email writing. The overarching principle to your correspondence should be clear and concise. Think about your own behaviours. When you receive long-winded, convoluted correspondence, do you get all excited about reading it and actioning it? No. You know that it'll take considered effort to digest and dissolve, so it won't get actioned immediately. Save the essays and verbal diarrhoea for your academic years to meet your word count. Let's go through the anatomy of an email and the key considerations in each:

- The subject line – when composing the subject line, think about it from the perspective that if you weren't around, and someone needed to find your correspondence, what would they search for? It needs to be descriptive enough for future reference. It's not ideal to start discussing new issues under an existing chain either unless you change the title. It's happened all too many times when a specific piece of advice or information was buried in a parallel chain and excessive sifting was required. Ensure to split unrelated points into separate, focused emails.

- The opening line – what is the purpose of this correspondence? This works to set the expectation or outline your request and should be direct and to the point. Establish the relevancy of the email to the reader and you have a higher chance of getting them to read it. If you are corresponding with someone for the first time, make sure you identify yourself clearly so they know who they're dealing with.

- The body – avoid the use of filler words and elongated sentences, as well as slabs of text. Ensure you have sufficient spacing between your sentences. Your language should be conversational, respectful and succinct. If you are unsure about the sentence length, read it out loud and see if you run out of breath. This is the part where you want to convey the information and key points, and each paragraph should contain one idea. This is a marker of coherent writing, where there is a flow and connection between your sentences.

- The close – this is your call to action. What do you want the reader to do and by when? Or is this email for their information only and you only need a read receipt? Check for completeness within your correspondence, ensuring that the recipient has all concrete information, direction or considerations they need to accurately respond.

I was tendering a package with a contractor who passed on a

complaint that a graduate he was dealing with on another project was being disrespectful and pulling rank on the contractor and engaging in poor tendering practices. Let's say they were drunk with the power of working for a head contractor. If you are a young gun working for a head contractor, you are not any better or superior than any consultant or subcontractor. I mention this because you must, in all forms of communication, be polite and respectful. It's a small industry, after all.

In the site sheds of the worst project I endured in my corporate career were signs hung overhead on the beams – *Communication is the key to success*. When I first got to this site, I was impressed that this was a site that would value communication and understood its relationship to establishing great project outcomes. It would also turn out to be the least communicative site in terms of transparency, openness and honesty, timeliness of information, consideration and expression of any sort of heart when it came to personal communication, and then some. Great communication only works in practice, not theory. The biggest misconception is that communication has happened, but the key to effective communication is if it's induced the intended outcome. In reflection, that site experience simply served as the greatest example of exactly how *not* to communicate with people around you if you wanted to have them respect you. Communication is by far the number one skill that if you were to master would yield you the greatest remuneration and progression in your career and life. Think about it. If you were to truly achieve a level of communication mastery, you would be able to enter any scenario and maintain a controlled outlook and steer the conversations that generate win-win outcomes. Except the last time that most people learnt how to speak was at the age of three, and that's when their learning and development on communication capped out. Assuredly, this shows in the workplace. Whilst a whole book can be written on communication (and there is ample literature as such), I will include in summary the key communication insights relevant to the current stage of your career. Let's start with concision:

- Anyone can get the point across in one thousand words, but not everyone can get the point across in one hundred words. The greatest orators aren't the ones who ramble on, lose their train of thought and go off into tangents. There is power in saying what you need to say clearly and in the least number of words.

- Listen, but not to respond. That's why speaking with concision helps, because all too many times people will zone out if you turn a five-minute conversation into a forty-minute one. When you are in conversation, be present and pay attention to what is being said and demonstrate that you are listening. This can be done by checking your understanding by repeating what was said. Being attentive to the person at hand shows respect, so where possible, avoid being on your phone at the same time.

- Get into the habit of taking notes of conversations. There will be times when issues turn into a he-said, she-said situation, and you want to have a timely record of any verbal agreements. If it is a direction or something which is binding, ensure that all verbal communication gets put into writing. This should be the same with internal team members who have given you a direction. You won't retain 100% of information and conversations that pass during your workday, which is diminished with time, so develop good note-taking habits.

- Learn construction industry jargon and acronyms. Even years on, I would be part of conversations that, based on the technicality that was spoken about, I would have no idea what was being said. I would simply take notes and follow up later for clarity. The first time you listen to a site manager discuss details with a subcontractor will appear to be a foreign language to you. But it is only through exposure that you will pick up the nuanced language of construction. The first acronym in the industry I learnt was RSD – can you guess what that is?

- Using communication as a tool isn't to diminish your presence because you may feel new or inexperienced. When speaking, there's no need to whisper and be invisible. There's no need to play down a request –'If it's okay with you I just …' There's also no need to be overly apologetic: 'Sorry, I just want to …' If you don't see yourself as someone worthy of having success, you will negatively use communication to play small and present yourself as small, unimportant and secondary.

Communication isn't about speaking and simple use of words, but connecting. How you say it, why you say it, when you say it, what you don't say and the non-verbal elements are all equally as important to the delivery of your message and establishing positive working relationships with those around you. You will find as you traverse corporate that most professionals can't speak, can't sell and can't connect. Therein lies your greatest window of opportunity. As composer John Powell said, 'Communication works for those who work at it.'

TRIGGER QUESTIONS

1. Are you confident in communicating in all scenarios?
2. What do you currently do well when it comes to communication?
3. What communication skills would you like to develop in the next twelve months?
4. How does your current communication make others feel?
5. How much time and development have you put into communication training in the last twelve months?
6. What do you think will be the consequence if you don't strategically develop your communication skills but leave it to chance?

YOUNG GUN BULLETS

- Become more expressive when you are talking. This means using more evocative body language and energy in your tonality and verbal delivery.
- Say what you need to say in the least number of words possible. Communication at a minimum needs to be clear and concise without the use of filler words. It needs to be concrete.
- Listen, but *really* listen. Empty your mind and remove distractions before going into conversations and be fully present with whom you are conversing with.

D

DETAIL

DĒ′TĀL″

AN INDIVIDUAL PART OR ITEM; A PARTICULAR;

A SMALL PART OF SOMETHING

'Little details have special talents in creating big problems!'
— Mehmet Murat İldan

It was in the first interview I had when I was looking to move into a contract administrator role where I first came across the lesson of the importance of attention to detail. The conversation was with the state manager, and I'd asked the question: what do your best graduates do that make them outstanding? He gave the example of one of the coordinators reviewing every single precast panel shop drawing, from ensuring that all panel drawings were provided in accordance with the panel layout plan, and then checking it against the structural drawings to ensure specific requirements like reo and penetrations were picked up. This enabled an efficient review process by consultants, who wouldn't get frustrated by missing drawings or details that they have already specified being missed by the contractors. This simple check is the role of a coordinator – otherwise a head contractor looks like a mailbox. When a consultant knows that the contractor has done a check and they don't have to waste their time with the trivial things, they'll also be more likely to get back to you in a timely manner. Why do I remember this six years after the fact? Because at the time, it seemed like something so simple to do, but then when I got into practice, I realised it's simple *not* to do, and is a true reflection of a good operator versus a brilliant operator– and someone who pays attention to detail or not.

A young gun will:

- Take the time to understand the detail of the design, methodology, installation, processes and so on with each respective trade of part of the project they are focusing on. This is applicable to all entry-level positions, not just those in a head contractor capacity. Slowing down to understand is imperative before you speed up your work processes and is what builds your technical expertise. And yes, despite pressing deadlines and everyone wanting something from you yesterday, if you don't take the time to understand the details then you will end up a paper pusher with superficial understanding of construction. For example, you can write a generic scope of works for tiling installation. Or you can add in the specific trade details that work to minimise the scope creep you may have later. Not investing in learning the details will catch up with you as your career progresses and you attain positions of seniority. It's not that you need to know it all, but there will be certain details that you are expected to know or know what questions to ask to get into the detail. You don't want to be caught out for silly mistakes as your career progresses. It reduces your competency and trust that others have in you.

- Check and double check their own work for consistency, especially for the little things. Are all pages attached in a contract when you submit it for review? Have you filled out all relevant cells in a comparison before you sit down for review? Have you checked all latest drawings are listed in the scope of works going out for tender? Have you reviewed the variation submission for all inclusions and listed all exclusions before it goes out? Have you checked the formatting on your 101 Excel sheets when printed? It's a hack that works despite how much I avoided it – print out your work and review a hard copy instead of a digital version. You will pick up on things that aren't immediately evident on-screen, as reading a physical copy forces you to slow down. As much as I hated multiple printout copies, it was a necessary evil for quality. Cross your 't's and dot your 'i's and check for completeness and cohesiveness of your work before having it reviewed by others. This was one of the best practice habits I had to be very conscious of, as I prefer speed and efficiency over perfection at times but worked to find the balance that would suit me and project stakeholders.

- Keep up-to-date and comprehensive records on any task at hand. This is the common analogy used in industry. If you were to be hit by a bus tomorrow (look both ways before crossing the road) would someone be able to come in and pick up your work where you left off? Consider the minimum standard of the quality of your project administration. Your records need to be detailed enough that if someone were to pick up your work and run with it, as they say, they will be able to do so without having much, if any, information missing. This means corresponding on project-sensitive information on the preferred platform, such as Aconex instead of emails. If you are away and someone else needs to follow up something on your behalf, they shouldn't need to chase you down to forward it. All relevant quotes or drawings should be on the server and not your desktop. It can be easy to get into sloppy bad habits early on, but in the same manner, you should ensure your record keeping is to a high standard from the outset to avoid issues later.

- Take the time to read construction documentation, and not simply attach it. It's a specific skillset that you develop in whatever entry-level position you hold. This includes, but isn't limited to, contracts, drawings, models, specifications, briefs and schedules. More often than not, when you ask a question to someone on your project team, they will first ask, 'What do the drawings say?' Sometimes the information you are seeking may be inferred in the documentation, but if you don't take time to familiarise yourself with it, you won't know it. In one of my podcast interviews, a managing director reflected on how she would read the specifications and briefs from cover to cover when she first started out, which surprised others. Why would you read it? So you can get familiar with the details, of course.

- Pay attention to the nuances and particulars of those that they work with. Every senior will have a preference as to how 'things should be done'. It can be from which shade of green they prefer and if numbers should be centrally aligned or to the left, who they wish to tender to or how they like their meeting minutes generated. It's these small preferences and pet peeves within people you are working under that are the hardest to change – there are some people who really do sweat the small stuff. Albeit there is nothing wrong with your work, as you are doing it based on what you were previously taught, there is a chance the new team and personnel you are working with will have an issue. Take the time to learn how your new team and manager like to get things done, from formatting to dealing with issues, as learning their details will enable you to constantly deliver quality work without excess rework.

- Don't get into the lazy habit of forwarding on correspondences without understanding them. For example, a subcontractor may send you a question on a detail. First, attempt to resolve it through the expertise onsite or in your team. If the proposed response needs consultant input, send them a new correspondence with the question and proposed solution. Don't forward on the original correspondence to the engineer and say, 'Please see below query from the concreter, can you please advise.' This just turns you into a simple mailbox, and anyone can become a forwarding service. The same when you get a response from the consultants. Make sure that the response fully responds to the original query. Before you send it on, you can call the contractor to discuss what the response was if needed. Again, don't send the response to the subcontractor and say, 'Please see response from the consultant.' If you are directing any other party to proceed on any basis, ensure that you understand what this means. Are there any financial implications? Is there a design change? Does the client or superintendent need to be notified? Does this design change impact any other trades? Do I need other trade or consultant input before proceeding? If you are ever unsure, ask the question before providing direction. In all instances, take the time to truly understand what is being asked so you don't become the master of the forwarding function.

> ## YOUNG GUN PRINCIPLE
> Take the time and patience to learn the details in every task you are given – technical or administrative. You can test your level of understanding by your ability to teach it to others to deliver on the same quality and outcome.

Your propensity towards thoroughness will reflect your high standard and commitment to your work, but will also require less supervision, even as a graduate. This confidence that your superiors will have in you, will allow you to put your hand up for more responsibility. The more that you can get exposure to in a shorter amount of time over and above your colleagues will, of course, put you in greater stead when you are seeking that next pay bracket, promotion or project. It's an artform to find the balance between managing the quality of your work versus the quantity of your work and competing demands, but those that do so are, of course, the young guns. You can also evaluate your own attentiveness to detail and wanting to perform exceptionally well on your tasks as a measure of your own engagement. If you find it's waning, and you don't care much anymore, it may be time to rethink if you are where you should be in your career.

> 'Most people don't have the patience to absorb their minds in the fine points and minutiae that are intrinsically part of their work. They are in a hurry to create effects and make a splash; they think in large brush strokes. Their work inevitably reveals their lack of attention to detail – it doesn't connect deeply with the public, and it feels flimsy.' – Robert Greene

There are, of course, personnel onsite who thrive on details and enjoy complexities, whereas others don't have the analytical mind or love for getting into the details. Either way, developing your technical aptitude is imperative in the first two to five years of your career. Thereafter, your career progression, remuneration and recognition doesn't rest on your technical laurels anymore. It is considered, but not the baseline or qualifier of decision-making when it comes to hiring, firing and promoting, and only accounts for 10% of your career success (higher if in medicine or science, for example). In any industry that you are in, reasonable competency is required and expected, but you should not isolate your development in the early years purely to the technical skillset of the work. If you have a myopic outlook from the start, you will miss investing in developing other skills that will be needed once you hit the four-to-five-year mark onwards. An exceptional young gun will seek to pursue holistic development of their mindset and skillset, well before it's required in the workplace.

TRIGGER QUESTIONS

1. Do you believe done is better than perfect? Why/why not?
2. Do you enjoy getting into the technical details?
3. Do you spend enough time understanding the details of your work instead of just becoming a paper pusher or a project inbox?
4. How do you make sure you consistently provide quality work?
5. What do you think are the most important characteristics for a detail-oriented person to have?
6. Based on your level of appreciation for detail, what type of projects do you think would suit you? For example, high-end fit-out has more details than an industrial complex.

YOUNG GUN BULLETS

- In the next response to an RFI (request for information), respond with a sketch or visual representation. Alternatively, provide a visual representation of a detail that has been verbally communicated to you to check your understanding.
- Participate in any design reviews where possible, and if you are tendering a package, conduct a detailed design review

with the relevant contractor. The more that you can get the expertise of others, the better you'll understand the design and construction process.

- Don't submit any work for review until you have reviewed it yourself twice. From checking your formatting to making sure all attachments are included, slow down and check your work before firing it off. As the old adage goes, measure twice, cut once.

E

EVALUATION

Ĭ-VĂL'YOO-Ā-SHUN

AN ASSESSMENT, SUCH AS AN ANNUAL PERSONNEL
PERFORMANCE REVIEW USED AS THE BASIS FOR A
SALARY INCREASE OR BONUS, OR A SUMMARY OF A
PARTICULAR SITUATION

---

*'The only thing worse than not requesting feedback
is not acting on it.' – Frank Sonnenberg*

I learnt that an absolute minority of people within corporate will go out of their way to give specific and timely feedback, be it positive or negative. Policy upon policy of how everyone needs to look out for each other, commit to integrity, and value progress and teamwork mean little when the simplest of requirements of people and performance management isn't executed to truly allow people to grow and excel. Positive feedback that gets relayed in real time works to reinforce an action and creates a positive association with the behaviour that the team would like to see. Constructive feedback that gets relayed in real time works to allow the recipient an opportunity to improve and tweak immediately, and a chance to respond or ask questions. There is little merit in bringing up a negative aspect of someone's performance in a performance review which can be months away, as it hasn't truly given the individual a chance to act on it. Whilst the former – being praise and reinforcement – is beneficial, the focus should be on constructive feedback, which is where the opportunity for growth happens. However, as most management staff are consumed in their own responsibilities, few will take the time to consistently evaluate your experience with you to provide consistent pointers for growth. The onus is on the young gun to seek out constructive feedback consistently and proactively, allowing them to refine and tweak their performance in real time. Otherwise, you may be waiting a long time for it to naturally come to you.

YOUNG GUN PRINCIPLE

Set up automatic reminders to ask for real-time weekly feedback and keep a record of the feedback received. Act on any calls for improvement immediately and seek feedback on that too.

It's important to be sponge-like and eager to learn, but when it comes to feedback, a level of discernment and assessment is important. Think of the following as having a sieve – the great feedback will be retained and the useless parts filtered through. For a young gun to take feedback onboard, and truly consider if its implementation will be beneficial, it needs to tick off the following criterion:

1. Feedback needs to be timely. If it is not provided in real time, then you are relying on someone's memory of an event, and over time this can come with human error and filtered with assumptions. 'Feedback should be offered as close as possible to the action in question,' says psychologist Victor Lipman. If it's not, the window of opportunity for rectification closes in.

• Specificity is key to delivering feedback. Which one of the following two sentences would you prefer to receive:
  – 'You need to pay more attention to detail.'
  – 'When you are combining contracts, first ensure that the latest version is being used. Then, check all the highlighted yellow cells and ensure they are filled out. Before you send it for review, print it out and check that all the latest appendices have been attached in order. We do this so our review time can be shortened, reduces your rework and allows the contract to be issued for review in a reasonable period.'

The latter, of course, which is specific, provides context and allows for actionable steps to be implemented to achieve the performance requirement. You cannot act on vague and nondescript directions and should put the onus on the person giving the feedback to explain further if you need clarification.

2. Feedback needs to be objective, not subjective. It's insufficient to receive feedback which is based on a feeling that is unsubstantiated. *What's the problem with this?* you ask. If someone is in a good mood, they'll give you a pat on the back. But when they are in a bad mood, are they still able to give you a pat on the back (if warranted)? Or are they going to give you negative feedback because of their mood? If their feedback changes like their mood, the goalposts are eternally moving, you can't win. If someone provides their perspective based on their feelings, then there is no baseline for truth in it. Feelings are subjective and can be interpreted a hundred different ways. When feedback on a feeling is provided, there is also no evidence. Whether it is positive or constructive feedback, you need objective evidence. If you're ever told, 'I feel that you're not doing a great job,' always ask for a specific example that demonstrates this. If no evidence can be provided to substantiate the claim, you'll never know how to improve. If you find yourself in a situation as such, have the backbone to stand up for yourself and respectfully request specific examples.

3. Feedback that encapsulates all the above should always have a future focus. Research by social behaviourists discovered that negatively focusing on someone's past behaviours won't cause them to change that behaviour moving forward. Instead, they'll spend more time trying to avoid punishment by covering up what they did wrong and avoid having formative conversations about it. There's no benefit in lamenting over what has been, so ensure that when you are on the receiving end of feedback, the outcome is focused on improving

future performance and outcomes and not dwelling on the past. If you find that you're receiving feedback with no plan for improvement, then question the intention of delivering it in the first place.

4. Feedback delivered needs to be about your performance and your outcomes, not the person. 'Never criticise the person. Always criticise the actions,' said Leo Babuata, author and zen teacher. In a train-wreck performance by previous management staff I worked with, the feedback provided was about a 'perception' that someone else onsite had of me. They'd missed the pivotal lesson that you cannot control someone's perception of you. What tangible and actionable steps can one take to appease someone else's perception? This feedback is about the person, not the action nor the outcome. It's none of your business what someone thinks of you. Before you take feedback onboard, ensure it is about an outcome and not about you personally.

'I think it's very important to have a feedback loop, where you're constantly thinking about what you've done and how you could be doing it better.' – Elon Musk

You may have found that most people will remember all the 'bad' things you have done, rather than the good things. Have you found in the company you keep that some people will be all too quick to remind you of a failure? 'That one time.' But they won't be so quick to list all the wonderful things you've done. This is simply human nature of those who possess a negative mindset that latches onto everything that hasn't gone right. And it won't be different in corporate. You may have volunteered your weekends to work, but the one mistake made along the way will find its way to your performance review. Most people will also not recall all the brilliant things you have done from last August, and it's likely neither will you. Therefore, the recommended practice for a young gun is this: have a physical or digital notebook available where you will log all the positive and constructive pieces of feedback you have received. If you get a 'good job' email from a client, store it in a feedback folder. Did you volunteer your weekends to supervise site? Log it. Did you negotiate a handsome contract sum? Log it. No matter how big or small the achievement, log it. This allows you to demonstrate exceptional performance over time, and this is hard to dispute. I assure you that at least once in your career you will find yourself working on a nightmare of a project, and you will need to have kept your own record of your performance and outcomes over time. Unfortunately, all the company policies on performance management mean very little if they're not abided by. I've seen and heard many graduates be told to move on with no forewarning. The purpose of record-keeping isn't only a safeguard for if things go pear-shaped, but just as useful for requesting pay increases or promotions, as you can objectively demonstrate high performance over time and have specific examples of all the work that you have done. I specifically remember making a note that on a variation I submitted where I managed to achieve a 12% margin, which was well above company average. I mentioned this in my performance review and achieved a larger pay rise as I was able to demonstrate that I have the commercial ability to add a multiple of value back to the company.

Remember, no-one but you will have the greatest vested interest in progressing your career – you need to drive it. And you need to be in a constant state of evaluation and regulation of self just as you expect those around you to lean in and provide you with feedback.

'The trouble with most of us is that we would rather be ruined by praise than saved by criticism.' – Norman Vincent Peale

TRIGGER QUESTIONS

1. Can you be more proactive in asking for feedback on a consistent basis?
2. Are you getting specific feedback to know what you need to be improving on?
3. Are you sensitive to receiving open and honest feedback? Do you have a positive relationship with receiving feedback and see it as constructive?
4. What's your current biggest challenge at work? Who has overcome this on your team that can assist?
5. Do you know what a mediocre person in your role would do versus an exceptional one? If not, who do you need to ask to get the profile of the ideal employee?
6. Do you know how to sift through feedback received that doesn't serve or align with your goals and ambitions? How would you respectfully reject feedback that you know won't serve you?

YOUNG GUN BULLETS

- Approach your manager and explain why consistent feedback is important to you. Set up a mutually agreeable time to have a constructive conversation about your progress and room for improvements. For example, a ten-minute conversation each Friday afternoon, and one formal sit-down conversation per month.
- Identify if there is anyone in your organisation that has the results you desire. Seek to set up a formal mentoring relationship. If there is no-one within your organisation, seek to get a mentor or a coach to aid your mindset and skillset development.
- Set time each week to reflect and evaluate your own progress against your goals. Don't just work *in* your career but *on* your career as well.

F

FINANCIALS

FƏ-NĂN'SHƏL

OF, RELATING TO, OR INVOLVING FINANCE,

FINANCES OR FINANCIERS

'Money is only a tool. It will take you wherever you wish,
but it will not replace you as the driver.'
— Ayn Rand

It was the one piece of advice I got from my past construction mentor when I was moving on from the first company that I worked for into a larger commercial builder. He told me to *know my numbers*. Up until then I'd worked as a project coordinator and had very little to do with the financial side of the project due to how the former company ran their projects. I remember feeling very overwhelmed in that moment, thinking, *I know nothing about the numbers*. Which numbers? What do I need to know? How will

I know which numbers I need to know? And only six months into my new position, it all made sense. In the building game, cash is king. There's no need to dance around the fact that companies are in it to profit. How they arrive to that outcome and how much of it they want to attain is discretionary. And numbers in construction do a lot of talking, which is why, regardless of your job title, you need to know it. Look to the world at large – if you want to see what's really going on, follow the money.

I was highly invested in the first commercial project I worked on, simply because I also loved the experience. With training, I was quickly in charge of the financial control of the project and was the go-to from all levels of management. What management are concerned with is accurate reporting of project financials, which has numerous repercussions upstream. When they ask an off-the-cuff question as to the status of a particular trade package or what profit margin you think will be reported, you need to answer them with confidence. To do so requires you to intimately know your numbers, and some of the best project administrators could tell you, down to the dollar value, how each trade package or cost code was performing. When the site manager came and asked for funding for a site requirement, I needed to know where it could be funded from without impacting the overall margin. Having a high level of financial control and responsibility during the early years of my career contributed to my fast progression, as being able to deliver to budget (without ignoring other aspects, of course) is a marker of your success as a project delivery personnel. The same principle would apply if you were working on the consultancy side. The client, whoever it is, always wants to be in the know as to where the project financials sit. That's why, as early on in your career as possible, you need to get close to the money on the project. On large projects, I have found that this is difficult to do, because the financial administration function is centralised to a few key people. It would be anarchy in the cost control system if several users were messing with the forecasts or adding in lines. This is a disadvantage to graduates who do start off on larger projects, because a key requirement of them typically getting promotions is exposure to project cost control. Therefore, even if the company doesn't make it a priority, *you* need to make it a priority to get as close to the financial control on a project as possible. The ability to forecast accurately is going to be supported by your exposure to site and level of technical aptitude that you develop, which will be discussed further on.

YOUNG GUN PRINCIPLE

Ensure that you get exposure to project financials and financial control as soon as possible in your career, and intimately get to know your numbers and the story that they are telling about the project outcomes.

It's not just accuracy that is a priority when it comes to talking numbers, but also creativity. As a project team, or the personnel closest to the numbers, how you represent the numbers is important. For example, there may be a large upcoming loss that you need to forecast or put on the risk and opportunity report. This should be offset with a forecast gain, so that the net moment is minimal and hopefully positive. There will be times when money issues arise, and you need to exercise creativity in your thinking as to how you present this to stakeholders. Once you report a positive or negative number, stakeholders tend to latch onto this, and it becomes the baseline of assessment. If you reported a loss of $100,000 but it ended up being $200,000, you can expect a serious grilling as to why this is the case. That's where your accuracy in the first place is required, teamed with a level of creativity to justify and explain why this is the case. For the same reason that stakeholders latch onto numbers quickly once reported, it's important as a project team that you can build in your own project contingency, so that when you need to 'move around some money' you can do so without impacting the bottom line. We call it putting money aside, and you'll need a level of creativity to do so, because if stakeholders saw a free pool of money, they'd rather bank it. It's through experience alone that you will become well versed in doing this, as well as talking about the numbers, but the better that you are at doing this, the more prized positions you may end up in, including the more recognised and challenging projects within a business.

Have you noticed how some executives hold coveted positions within a construction business but have no construction background? If you look at the trajectories of chief financial officers, for example, they typically have accounting, tax or financial consultancy experience. They learn the nuances of construction along the way, but a balance sheet is a balance sheet. They first and foremost understand money, and as I said, businesses are in the game for a reason. Ensure that as your career progresses, your outlook of financials isn't myopic purely to the project(s) you are working on but to the business at large. The better you are at understanding and managing money and the closer that you are to the flow of it in an organisation, the faster you will be able to progress in your career. Why do you think highly technical people, no matter how brilliant they are, are not the ones at the executive or leadership level? Technical aptitude only takes you so far, after that, you're looking at a high-income skillset, and what is more high-income of a skillset than being able to bring in the income?

'Many people take no care of their money till they come nearly to the end of it, and others do just the same with their time.'
— Johann Wolfgang von Goethe

As a young gun, you will make many mistakes when it comes to reporting numbers, tendering, negotiating, orders, the whole host. I still remember the exact value and scope gaps on packages I let that cost tens of thousands of dollars. I missed the fine print on the bluestone tiles that the subcontractor quoted on, that they weren't the specified tile but an alternative equivalent. Unfortunately, the alternative equivalent wasn't approved, and we had to fork over the extra to get the specified tile. I have since checked every tile I have ever ordered. The very first trade package I let was brickwork. Brickwork per square metre is costly, so even a few extra metres here and there adds up quickly. I was hit with a $50,000 variation for extra brickwork of walls and heights that changed during the design process. Whilst there was partial merit, the contractor also didn't abide by the variation notice periods, and simply undertook the work onsite without telling anyone in good faith. We ended up meeting in the middle. I remember these examples years on, as will you. I share this to show it's okay to make mistakes – it's how you learn – but we don't want to be making the same mistakes twice. That's why paying attention to detail is key because details in construction more often than not have money associated with them. The key is to also take ownership and responsibility. I felt awful, in the moment, fronting up that I didn't read the fine print on the tiles, but I felt great afterwards that I took ownership, and the project manager commended me on doing so. The first few times you're reviewing a claim, awarding words or approving invoices, you will be flying blind. First ensure that you understand where this financial document sits in the overall scheme of project financials, don't just plug in numbers into a software. Understanding the context is key first before you can understand the tactical side of each type of document. Don't try and rush through any of these reviews, take time for sound assessment and understanding of financial documents.

Due to the sequence of works, the entrance to an administration building I was working on needed these feature timber LVLs (laminated veneer lumber) installed, and we weren't anywhere near awarding a carpentry package. I got the contact of a subcontractor who was dragging his feet in giving me a price. He could tell I was new and made the works out to be the most complicated installation. I got a quote weeks later to supply and install twenty-eight feature LVLs for $28,000. I had no baseline for assessing the complexity of the work, but the site manager said this was absurd. I ended up buying the material direct from the supplier and paying two contractors on day labour to install it, totalling about $4,000. It takes time to build up your own reference library as to what certain works should cost. Even if you're starting as a quantity surveyor, you will learn all the same, as Rawlinsons has its limitations. There are people onsite that could tell you a fair and reasonable rate or ballpark figure of what works should cost. Ensure that you lean into their experience and financial acumen to reduce mistakes and certainly avoid overpaying. Start developing that library of how long things should take, what's involved and what's a fair and reasonable assessment. This will come from site exposure and also asking questions to personnel with experience around you. When you also develop great rapport with contractors, they will quickly be able to give you up-to-date rates for materials and the like, which is ultimately the best resource. When you are seeking to get just about anything approved, management or your client-side project manager will want to see your assessment of the rate or the breakdown of the price to ensure it is fair and reasonable. Get into the habit of challenging every rate, variation and submission early on. Don't just take it to be correct on face value. The point of this isn't only to reduce the cost (a bonus), but in doing so, you may find out that a key component of the works hasn't been accounted for, possibly costing you more later. I was always told by contractors that my approach was fair and reasonable. It's hard to argue with someone if they are being just that – fair *and* reasonable. This comes from building your own mental library for what things should cost.

YOUNG GUN PRINCIPLE

Question and check all pricing and claims that come through to the extent that if someone were to challenge you on its validity, you could support the figure with confidence.

The more proficient you are with numbers, the stronger your position to negotiate. You need to know the parameters and where you can move to when it comes to a negotiation. Do you have room to move? As sometimes, for the benefit of the relationship, a variation or rate will need to go through. There are things on projects that are worth more than money. When you know how much room you have to move, you'll be in a better position to negotiate and come to mutually beneficial outcomes. There is a rife tendency in the construction culture to 'screw down' anyone else to make money. There is little skill involved in telling someone to drop their price or they won't get the work. You can't be relying on authority to negotiate alone. It's a skill that can be developed at any level and one that has more and more pressing need as you move into managerial and leadership positions. Unfortunately, the manager that a graduate works under will distinctly shape how they approach negotiations. Most take the bullish approach of screwing down the other party. Of course, this would be eradicated if the process from the start of tendering from the clients would improve. Alas, we are far from a utopian version of construction. Remember that all parties contracted to a project have the right to make a profit, and the approach taken to negotiations should be win-win, not, win for one and burn the relationship and lose moving forward.

TRIGGER QUESTIONS

1. Are you aware how project finances contribute to corporate finances?
2. Do you know where the biggest financial risks are on the project?

3. Do you keep your own rates library? If not, start doing so.

4. How confident are you explaining project financial concepts like forecast cost to completion (FFC) orrisk and opportunity (R&O) to a new graduate? Write out your own understanding of these terms.

5. Do you feel confident discussing rates and pricing with relevant stakeholders? If not, what can you do to increase that confidence and acumen?

6. Do you understand larger financial systems, where money comes from and the relationship it has with value? Do you feel that you spend enough time truly understanding money?

YOUNG GUN BULLETS

- Ask to join the next cost report review meeting and take notes on the questions asked by corporate management. The more understanding you have of what they're looking for, the better reports you'll generate.

- Put your hand up to be involved in a start-to-finish tendering process and then be tasked with the financial administration of said contractor. If you get push-back, ask what the avenues for you are to get exposure to this as soon as possible.

- Sit with the financial administrator or controller for one hour a month when they generate the progress claims and cashflow, so you can start to generate big-picture financial acumen. Ensure you discuss this with your management team and itemise how this won't impact your current workload.

G

GROUPWORK

ˈgRUːP ˌW3ːK

A TECHNIQUE WITHIN THE FIELD OF SOCIAL WORK
WHEREIN VARIOUS GROUPS ARE GUIDED BY AN
AGENCY LEADER TO MORE EFFECTIVE PERSONAL
ADJUSTMENT AND COMMUNITY PARTICIPATION

---

*'We can work together but we can't just work with each
other.'*
– Oscar Auliq-Ice

Remember those tedious group assignments at university? There
was always one person who either didn't do any work or started
at the eleventh hour before the assignment was due. On the other
end of the spectrum, there was the group leader, who organised
times to meet, worked to deadlines and made sure the assignment
got across the line. I hope if you are reading this, you are the

latter, not the former. Whilst groupwork was common during your academic experience, no-one actually teaches you how to manage group scenarios and task units. Whilst it's imperative that you can work independently, you also need to start versing yourself with group cohesiveness, dynamics and behaviour to ensure that, above all, project outcomes are met. Maybe at work you've joined the social committee or you are temporarily put into a task-specific team – you can leverage the insight to position yourself as a team leader and create the opportunity for yourself to demonstrate your great organisational and leadership ability.

YOUNG GUN PRINCIPLE

Use group situations to drive performance by cultivating cohesiveness and true inclusivity and demonstrate your leadership capability.

When you've found yourself working in a new group, whether recently formed or established, we want to see group cohesiveness. When groups are formed, cohesiveness is imperative to drive success on outcomes. The following insights can be implemented at any level of the group to foster cohesiveness. A common misconception by group leaders is that group members know what their collective mission is. The common aim or purpose isn't only to be reiterated at the start, but at every group gathering. Eight years of corporate team, client and site meetings and only on very few occasions was the collective purpose reinstated. The goal of the group should be clearly established at the start and reiterated at every chance to meet. It takes over twenty-seven times for a marketing message to be repeated before it becomes memorable, and that is ever increasing in a world full of distractions. You can never over-explain a vision, only under-explain it. If you are tasked with establishing the group in the first place, knowing the objective prior to its formation is key, as this will inform who should be on the team and give them an opportunity to assess if they would like to be. Establishing group cohesion is also founded on taking the time to understand the strengths and weaknesses of each member. You can outright ask this, as you are better off steering each group member to work to their strengths. Take advantage of each person's natural talents and disposition, instead of random allocation of work. When groups form, they also form norms, which are preferred ways of working. One thing that should be a baseline is for clear, transparent and timely communication. Little else frustrates group members than when they aren't kept in the loop. And when the group does come together, ensure that the wins are celebrated – this is a key norm to establish from the outset, as it works to reinforce the desired behaviour. Recognition is an innate human need, so before getting straight to business when the group comes together, publicly celebrate the wins. You want to celebrate in public but provide constructive criticism privately.

In groups, there is always the dominant individual, which can leave others feeling like they don't have space at the table. Ensure that a culture of true inclusivity is fostered, so that all can openly share their thoughts. Encouraging interaction could be as simple as extending an invitation to the quietest and asking them, 'What do you think?' If a person is on a team, they need to play an active role in it, and the most dominant may not see this. This will keep them group bound instead of feeling external to it. As a young gun, you can start observing group cohesiveness and actively making suggestions to improve how groups can stick together for success.

For where there are people, there are problems. Problems cannot exist if there are no people involved. It's inevitable in your career trajectory that you'll be part of groups that lack cohesiveness despite all well-intentioned efforts, as you are dealing with the greatest variabilities of them all: personalities. There are five key sources in groupwork where cohesiveness will be impacted: conflict, non-participation and withdrawal, monopolising and scapegoating. Let's go into detail in each:

- Conflict is when personnel in a group clash in perspectives. This isn't an issue as it allows for open dialogue, but it becomes an issue when people attack the person and not the problem. There are three types of conflicts. One is about information misunderstanding, where misinformation has been presented that hasn't yielded beneficial outcomes. The second type of conflict stems from values misalignment. Your manager may value work and you may value family, so when you leave work on time, they may perceive this as not getting the work done (which is hopefully incorrect). There's a mismatch in values and misunderstanding between people when they value different things. The key is to recognise what both want within the group. The third type is when someone doesn't want to agree with you. This could stem from varying factors, such as background agreements or personal vendettas, but it presents unwillingness to come to the party. When you are faced with conflict in a group scenario, it is worth placing it into context to properly address the issue, and not vilify the person immediately.

- Non-participation and withdrawal are when an individual in a group is hesitant to contribute, and this could stem from a multitude of factors. They may lack self-confidence, lack the skillset to carry out the task, lack the time or may not want to be part of the group. Selection and assessment of group members up-front can aid to mitigate this. Talking to group members who are withdrawn to understand their behaviour will also aid cohesiveness in the long-term.

- Monopolising is when one person in the group, quite frankly, takes up all the space in the group, and it's their way or no way. The best strategy is to first discuss this with the dominant individual, by explaining that if others had a chance to contribute, there would be collectively better outcomes. Approaching this in a way that doesn't dampen their involvement is key.

- Scapegoating occurs in a group when things haven't gone to plan and members are seeking to shift the blame and point the finger to others. The individual certainly needs to take extreme ownership for their actions, but the group is also responsible. Instead of seeking to shift the blame, refocus on identifying how this can be avoided moving forward and focusing on solutions.

'Cooperation is the thorough conviction that nobody can get there unless everybody gets there.' – Virginia Burden

By recognising the types of friction that may arise in group situations, you are better positioned to deal with the situations by identifying the root cause. This will demonstrate your critical thinking, but also leadership capability, even if you're not the official head of the team. Making assumptions within teams to resolve conflicts is like attempting to walk through a minefield hoping to get it right. Use the art of questioning to diffuse these situations and remain solutions-focused. The groups that perform well over the long run are those where the individual isn't lost or compromised in the process of the group achieving outcomes but can see how the collective will benefit themselves and the project. Differences in groups should also be nurtured, as a dangerous territory to enter is groupthink – where everyone thinks uniformly and is always unanimous. Differences should be valued as it's where innovation, different solutions and different ways of thinking can be put forth.

TRIGGER QUESTIONS

1. What are the greatest challenges you see when working in groups?
2. What is one change you could make in the way you listen to others that would improve your effectiveness in working in a group?
3. If you could pick one person in the group to give a specific compliment about their work, who would it be and what would you say?
4. What are three strategies you can implement to build group cohesiveness?
5. What role do you naturally gravitate towards in teams? What does this say about the value you bring?
6. Do you get intimidated easily in group scenarios? Why do you think this is the case?

YOUNG GUN BULLETS

➨ Generate a team mission statement and suggest for it to be read out at the start of every group meeting.

➨ Give specific positive feedback to a member of your team during each meeting.

➨ Ask if you can chair each team meeting, to enable everyone at the table a chance to participate, but also for you to take the organisational lead.

H

HARD WORK

HĀRDWÛRK
SOMETHING REQUIRING LOTS OF EFFORT TO DO,
EITHER PHYSICALLY, MENTALLY OR EMOTIONALLY;
LABOUR; TOIL

'It's hard to beat a person who never gives up.'
– George Herman Ruth

There is no antidote to hard work at the start of your career, but what is it exactly? Hard work by a conventional definition would be lifting blocks up stairs on a thirty-degree day. Hard work would be having to dig trenches by hand. Hard work is building a business atop your sixty-hour corporate job. Hard work can be perceived as doing the work that others won't do. What you do at work is just work. Not hard work. Pulling long hours at work isn't hard work, it's just long hours. All your chores, daily obligations and what you need to do as a minimum to keep yourself and home in order isn't hard work, it's just regular work. Every human being does this, and it doesn't make them hard workers. Hard work is what you do atop of all the regular work and regular things you do (inside and outside of work) that you've chosen to take on to achieve your goals.

Then why is hard work imperative to success? Hard work also encapsulates focused and consistent work that goes over and above the average expectations and requirements. When you put in the hard work up-front, you're prepared for opportunities when they knock. Success doesn't just show up one day because you've been doing the minimum for the last few years. Think about the life of an elite athlete. Their work isn't just what happens on the courts or during their training sessions. They spend hours in meal preparation, optimising their mind, body and training regime. Every waking hour of their day is an extension of what they do. When championships come, they're ready. Their hard work is their default status so they can perform and win. Hard work, to some, becomes an obsession; you can be the judge of whether that's positive or otherwise. Hard work in the pursuit of your ambition is something that is done all the time, and this is what works to build discipline. You can't be interested in success, you need to be committed, and this does require sustained levels of effort. There is also no achievement truly worth having that comes into fruition without hard work, and it requires application of your mind, body and soul. It's why when people start to stretch themselves, they improve in every arena. Especially when it comes to the tenacious, cannot-get-me-down mindset that comes with the rigour of hard work. And with this comes confidence in knowing that you can outwork most – not in quantity, but quality. Those who shy away from sweat equity have resigned to mediocre careers and lives. You only need to look to your immediate circle to see people locked into their nine to five on repeat – that's not a stretch, that's actually a boring life if you were to watch it in replay. If someone is just focused on survival, they cannot be focused on winning at the same time.

YOUNG GUN PRINCIPLE

To work smart, you must first work hard. There is no way to bypass the sweat equity to achieve your goals and ambitions, for success doesn't come without it.

Should you work harder than your colleagues? As an ambitious person in corporate, you will find that most people will do the bare minimum and expect the absolute maximum. It's not for you to lower your standards and modus operandi to suit others, but for others to raise theirs to meet yours. The long-term consequence of you getting lax and putting your drive on low because of those around you will diminish your long-term prospects and render you incapable of pursuing anything greater than average. You're not working hard for your colleagues; you're doing it for *you.* And don't be surprised that one day you will come to the realisation that if you're going to put in so much effort, you may as well do it for your own business, instead of doing it to build someone else's. Remember, no-one is going to demand high standards from you, it must come from within. I assure you that quality managers and leaders don't let this go unseen.

'I'm a great believer in luck, and I find the harder I work the more I have of it.' – Thomas Jefferson

As a young gun with an insatiable work ethic, you'll more likely than not be rewarded with more responsibility. Isn't that a great paradox – the reward for hard work is more hard work. Consider this an opportunity to diversify your skillset, gain more exposure and experience within a period, and add to your achievement list and highlight reel. When additional responsibilities do come your way, ensure that you are managing priorities and expectations (refer to O for Organisation).

TRIGGER QUESTIONS

1. Are you defining productivity and hard work the right way?
2. Are you addicted to being busy and not productive?
3. Do you put in consistent effort instead of sporadic effort to produce outcomes? Which do you think is more conducive to success?
4. What's the difference in your role between hard work and smart work?
5. Reflect on past situations in your life where hard work has paid off. How can you apply the same ethic to achieve your greater goals today?
6. Have you been consistent in your efforts, or sporadic? Do you find that you give up too soon or stay for the long haul? Why/why not?

YOUNG GUN BULLETS

- Identify the key distractions during your day and eliminate them. You may need to put timers on social media or avoid getting a coffee in the kitchen if you know you'll waste ten minutes talking. You will increase the time you have for sustained, focused work.

- Avoid multitasking. Our brain cannot complete more than one task at a time. It's not considered multitasking to be jumping between tasks. Do tasks in a stop and start manner rather than five tasks half-heartedly.

- Optimise your environment for focused periods of work. Ensure your environment is comfortable and distraction free, and work in intense time blocks with breaks. The 'pomodoro' technique has you set a timer for twenty-five minutes of distraction-free, focused work with a five-minute break. Your brain performs better in blocks rather than elongated periods of time with sporadic effort.

I

INTELLIGENCE

ĬN-TĔL'ə-JƏNS

THE ABILITY TO ACQUIRE, UNDERSTAND

AND USE KNOWLEDGE

'It takes something more than intelligence to act intelligently.'
— Fyodor Dostoevsky

Person A is a senior within an organisation earning $250,000, who doesn't have the trust and respect of their colleagues, engages in unethical behaviour, but has been in the industry for twenty years and has several degrees.

Person B runs their own company coming from a trade background, gets to work on great projects inside and outside of their business, and invests a considerable amount into their mind, body and soul. However, they find themselves working too much.

Who is more intelligent?

There is no immediate right answer in this instance because you are missing many metrics to measure this. However, I want to highlight that under the guise of degrees, experience and job titles alone, will most people claim to be intelligent. With Person A, I find a person who doesn't have vision, self-awareness or evolved consciousness to be intelligent at all. What they may be is technically brilliant, but success or growth in one arena that doesn't translate to holistic success or growth in all arenas of their life, cannot be considered true intelligence. Intelligence also comes from knowing, and building on your knowledge happens through discovering things for yourself. Most people believe things based on belief instead of discovery. They haven't gone out of their way to critically think, explore, compare, evaluate, challenge, dissect. They haven't proven that they can think outside thoughts that have been determined for them. You'll become a far more evolved individual if you speak from experience rather than theory. Those who claim that they already know all they need to know are proving that they aren't aware of their own blind spots and are operating out of the egotistical mind which doesn't allow them to experience advanced intelligence.

I've spoken to industry professionals who may have fifteen years 'experience', but when I asked them what they're seeking to achieve in their career, they couldn't answer. I've spoken to people who display low levels of critical thinking and inability to cross-examine their own thinking process but are seniors in organisations. I've spoken to and mentored graduates who have a heightened sense of awareness to their thinking and foster a deep spiritual connection all the same. Intelligence has nothing to do with seniority or tenure – agree or disagree now? Most people have also proven that they can't think and won't think, so they can try and prove their intelligence to you all they want, but alas, it's missing. This is a harsh truth that many simply don't want to hear, because it touches their ego. Now, I'm being matter-of-fact with you as I'm in the business of thinking, as a Thought Leader. We are all in the business of thinking, for the quality of your thoughts determine the quality of your life outcomes. And it's not to say that I'm better. Spiritually, we are all equal. Only when an individual goes on the self-discovery journey to deconstruct and reconstruct their own paradigms, beliefs, persona and start seeking knowledge, will they start to have a degree of differentiation from the collective intelligence found. As a young gun, you need to have conscious awareness that intelligence doesn't only concern itself with how competent you are at your job. Psychology has provided many theories as to what constitutes intelligence. American psychologist and psychometrician Robert Sternberg sees intelligence comprising of three parts (triarchic theory of intelligence):

- Analytical intelligence – academic problem-solving and computation.
- Creative intelligence – imaginative and innovative problem-solving.
- Practical intelligence – street smarts and common sense.

Where most people solely concern themselves is analytical intelligence, because conventional academic and corporate institutions have generated the false belief that that's all there is. We can see that it's not. I chose I for Intelligence because whilst it may seem common practice, it's not. Most people only have an illusion of knowledge and illusion of intelligence. It's not the same as actually being intelligent. A young gun must keep developing their knowledge strategically and not sporadically in order to truly elevate their consciousness so they can stand out and succeed. Success or differentiation doesn't happen when you think like everyone else. If you think like everyone else, you will also have the same results as everyone else. Look around your immediate circle – do you really want their results?

YOUNG GUN PRINCIPLE

Developing a deep understanding of human psychology, why people do what they do, the faculties of your mind and how you think will enable you to have a sharp edge and expanded consciousness that will greatly influence your career and that of others.

As complex as the frameworks and theories on intelligence are, I find the seven levels of intelligence, as reflected in colour psychology, give a holistic introduction to the layers of intelligence. I bring this to your attention because as a young gun, your growth and mental cognition needs to be developed holistically. Plus, different scenarios, professionally and personally, that you will come across will require you to use different types of intelligence. I can't approach a client who is stuck with the same intelligence used in a business and planning meeting. Dr Max Luscher, Swiss psychotherapist, brought colour psychology into the modern world over fifty years ago, and it was further brought to fruition by Christopher Hills, author of *Nuclear Evolution*. The colours refer to each of our biological energy centres. The seven levels of intelligence per Hills are:

1. **Physical intelligence (red):** this is our ability to read and understand our surroundings through our five senses and know how to take care of our bodies through maintaining our health. Whilst many may appear to be great at work, that won't matter much if their health fails them. And when it does, you can be sure they'll say they wish they took more care of it. Remember, you live in your body, it's the only home your spirit has. Pay close attention to your stress and energy levels, and learn to leave the demands of work at work, before they seep into every crevice of your life until you don't even recognise your life outside of work.

2. **Social intelligence (orange):** this is your ability to relate and understand yourself in association to the relationship you have with others. This level of intelligence focuses on your ability to nurture and maintain relationships (professional and personal) and how you approach certain people by understanding them. Think of your social intelligence as your ability to read the room and know what to say, when and to whom. As a young gun, it may not be wise to approach your site manager, who is dealing with a safety issue onsite, to sit with you to review a complex issue.

3. **Intellectual intelligence (yellow):** this is your analytical and rational ability to look at information, distil it, store it and know when to use it. It's the intellectual part which allows you to problem-solve, think sequentially and logically, identify when something may be amiss and take

a balanced approach to making a judgement call. Your logical mind will be the one to identify that shop drawings need to be sent to approval, through to a meeting between relevant stakeholders which needs to be held to discuss a complex design detail.

4. **Emotional intelligence (EQ) (green):** emotional intelligence is concerned with the ability to understand the emotions of yourself and of others, regulating your own emotions, paying attention to what isn't being said and knowing when to extend empathy. People with a heightened sense of EQ are found to have well-developed social skills. This is intelligence that is concerned with the heart and deals with feelings. Humans are fundamentally emotive beings, and you won't get into any sort of leadership position if you wholly rely on logic (intellectual intelligence) to see you through complex situations. EQ can be demonstrated in the smallest of ways. When a person on a team is expressing that they're burning out, the response is to listen to what they are experiencing and not immediately conclude that it's a time-management issue.

5. **Conceptual intelligence (blue):** the conceptual mind can take loose pieces of information and form mental models around it. It also deals with memory, ideas and concepts. My conceptual mind allowed me to come up with the framework of this book. I considered how to piece together all the loose and varied experiences and lessons, to find that an A-Z guide would best allow me to do that in a structured way. The conceptual mind will take a chaotic sequence of reviewing drawings and systemise it so that everyone on the team can be following the same process, for example.

6. **Intuitive intelligence (indigo):** this is the 'knowing' type of intelligence that is driven by our intuition. This is the type of intelligence that allows us to be divinely guided and is strengthened through our connection to source (whatever you identify as source for yourself). Were there times in your life where you just *knew* you had to take a position? That you just *knew* you had to move halfway round the world? There are decisions that can't be logically justified, but all your being knew it's what had to be done.

7. **Imaginative intelligence (violet):** the most expansive and infinite of them all. Our imaginative intelligence is our highest form of intelligence that deals with invention and innovation, and to see alternative ways of being and doing within our own mind's eye. The professional world has been trained to turn off this intelligence, and it shows in the lack of creativity in the lives that many lead. The conception of this book, in the first instance, required my imagination and then my intuition to know that this is what I should write about. I then reverted to my intellectual mind to rationally plan how I would go about bringing this to light. All creation comes from imagination, which is infinite and boundless in what you can conceive.

Whilst all types of intelligences are important, I will expand on EQ. First understand that everyone is an emotional being. No matter how tough and logical someone may appear on the surface, they are still emotionally driven. When I was navigating my way through corporate, I noticed the status quo being highly disconnected from their heart set. I found, through my experience, that few took the time to understand the person and reverted to simple processes to deal with situations. Some were just simply uncaring and lacked human compassion, seeing others as a disposable resource. Noticing that workplaces were devoid of emotions, I worked supremely hard at suppressing all emotions, not wanting to connect to my own feelings as there was no space for them in the workplace. I look back now, thinking what a robotic existence it must have been. Not only was this damaging for me, but in the same merit, I could never truly connect with someone based on an intellectual connection alone. The greatest transformation I had was letting go of the notion that emotions are all bad and that there is no space for them in my career. EQ refers to the ability to perceive, control and evaluate emotions, which is essential in corporate environments despite it never truly being fervently on display. There's the difference between observing your emotions and not being consumed by it. When the majority get the two mixed up they end up displaying nothing or being debilitated by what they feel. As a young gun, it's imperative that you don't discount emotions but learn to navigate them, in yourself and others. Research conducted with Fortune 500 CEOs by the Stanford Research Institute International and the Carnegie Melon Foundation found that 75% of long-term job success depends on people skills, while only 25% on technical knowledge. It's not just promotions that benefit, but also pay. EQ-i found that people with high EQ make $29,000 more annually than people with low EQ. The key to developing your EQ is to truly understand the perspective of another person, which is done via listening and asking questions. If you conclude too quickly, falsely assume something about the other person, or even worse, put words in their mouth, there will be an immediate disconnect. Being the person who can listen and foster heartfelt connections that is a cause of you truly caring about the people around you will significantly increase your success and potential.

'The difference between intelligence and education is this: intelligence will make you a good living.' – Charles F Kettering

This may come as a surprise to many, but not everyone thinks like you do. What may seem obvious to you, may seem crazy to someone else. Whilst you may see the world through facts and figures, someone else may see the world through pictures and stories. Intelligence is also about understanding and thinking about how others are thinking. To truly connect with the other person, you'll use your intelligence to marry the two. This may sound complex at first, but stay with the thought. It takes a sharpened level of intelligence to see and understand the world view of others. No-one is going to tell you outright how they see the world, it will be up to your perceptiveness to pick up on the nuances in their words, behaviours and responses to understand this. I mention this because most people only care about themselves and what's relevant and pressing in their world. This won't make you a great manager, let alone a leader, and will leave you locked in the modality of an average employee. No-one will tell you that this is what you need to develop to standout, because only the sharpest of executives in corporate do this. The way you perceive reality isn't the only version of reality that exists.

The professional world, nor the conventional academic world, doesn't teach you any of this. It only teaches you what to think, not how to think. There is no situation you will experience that is immune from understanding human behaviour and knowing what type of intelligence is applicable. It's imperative that you invest in the development of your mindset from now until the end of time, for you don't want to become an intellectual idiot – a term coined by my mentor, Ron Malhotra.

TRIGGER QUESTIONS

1. Do you believe that success can only come from your credentials and experience?
2. How quickly can you adapt to changing realities?
3. Do you quickly reject new ideas, or can you sit with the discomfort of the unknown?
4. How often do you test your own belief system? Do you know if your belief system is serving you or hindering you?
5. Are you aware of how thoughts are formed? Do you spend time in reflection on your own thoughts?
6. Do you know the difference between intelligence and wisdom? What do you think the difference is and how does this benefit the quality of your career and life?

YOUNG GUN BULLETS

- Read one book a week for the next twelve months on a variety of topics – spirituality, money, entrepreneurship, success and so on. Reading wires your brain for higher intelligence. You can do this via Audible or get a physical hard copy to meet your targets.

- Start a ten-minute daily journalling practice to get into the habit of thinking about what you have learnt and to get familiar sitting in reflection with your own thoughts. Challenge your own thinking by asking more questions to yourself to dig deep to your levels of intelligence.

- Start a daily meditation practice to learn how to observe and control your thoughts. This peace and tranquillity is crucial to building intellect and making space for new thoughts. A mind riddled with fear and doubt doesn't seed great ideas.

J

JUDGEMENT

JŬJ'MƏNT

THE COGNITIVE PROCESS OF REACHING A DECISION
OR DRAWING CONCLUSIONS

'Fortune truly helps those who are of good judgement.'
– Euripides

A contractor who has beaten program wants additional payment in their December claim to cover offsite material deposits. The material deposit is to be paid before the Christmas shutdown period. Contractually, payment for offsite material isn't a condition of contract. And to rush through payment this side of Christmas would require a discount from the contractor. However, up-front you already heavily negotiated the tender sum with a handshake promise that there wouldn't be any further significant discounts. What would you do? One line of approach is to take the hard contractual line, another is to take the amicable relationship approach based in good faith, and the final option is to find a middle ground. Which do you take? What would be considered fair in this scenario?

Let's look at another scenario. You're the lead young gun in your team, and you see the project manager being unjustly harsh to another team member when their performance is equal to yours. Do you say anything? If you say something, the heat could turn on you (refer to P for Politics). If you don't say anything, are you then accepting mediocre standards in the workplace? Remember, the standards you walk by are the standards you accept.

Last scenario: you're tendering a package, and one contractor is a great industry contact of yours. The other has put in a quality submission, competitive price, and for all intents and purposes, is an apple-for-apple comparison. Both contractors need the work, and your industry contact is calling you daily for the work. Will you be swayed by personal affinities? Or will you hold an objective, best-for-project outlook? What's the best-case outcome and worst-case outcome for each?

Judgment is the ability to combine personal qualities with relevant knowledge and experience to form opinions and make decisions–this is also at the core of exemplary leadership according to Noel Tichy and Warren Bennis (the authors of *Judgment: How Winning Leaders Make Great Calls*). However, as you can see, not all situations are clear cut, but regardless of what is in front of you, you are required to exercise great judgement. The root cause of lack of quality judgements is that most people can't think or won't think, and don't have conscious awareness that they are in charge of their own thoughts.

> ## YOUNG GUN PRINCIPLE
> Both the mind and the heart are essential to making great judgement calls, and a young gun will make great judgements based on this and the highest consideration for morality and ethics.

How do you then develop good judgement? And what is considered good judgement? What I deem as good may not be what is good to you. Contrary to popular belief, judgement doesn't always have to be fair or unanimous. For example, a male and a female are working in equivalent roles, with equivalent workloads. The male counterpart significantly out-performs the female counterpart. Is it fair they still get paid equally? I can imagine the contention this will stir up, and yes, there are further considerations to the example. Fairness without earning it is entitlement, and no-one owes you any-thing. Developing good judgement is also predicated on being able to suspend your belief system. Severe bias comes through when people pass judgement.

Take the above tendering scenario. It can be easy for some-one without moral and ethical standing to simply give the project to their friend to maintain relationship harmony. They may be biased by the history with this contractor instead of taking an objective view. A healthy level of critical thinking, detachment and scepticism of your biases is necessary and a difficult skill to master. There are certain scenarios where you can apply quick logic to pass judgement. Should I eat this sugary item to overcome the 3pm slump? Probably not. There are more complex scenarios where the need to rush and come to a decision where quick logic doesn't apply, but slow logic is the right practice. For example, you may be responsible for an underperforming cadet. Before judging that they're lazy, dig deeper. They might be uninspired or disengaged. Avoiding jumping to conclusions is imperative to sound judgement. Great judgement also comes from experience. To gain more experiences (*experiences*, not *experience*, note the difference) requires you to actively seek new scenarios and take new risks so you can increase your bandwidth of experiences. If you rely on your workplace to provide you with diversity of experience alone, you're leaving an insane amount of opportunity on the table. We all have an inner guidance system, like cars have a GPS. At times, to extend sound judgement, following a gut feel after critically assessing all the relevant data and information may be the only course of action. Your intuitive faculties will only get stronger the more you listen to them, not by constantly going against them. American actor Will Rogers said, 'Good judgement comes from experience and experience comes from bad judgement.' Fear not making bad judgements, but only fear making no judgement at all.

To exercise good judgement then, a young gun needs to make their decisions and judgement calls strongly based within their core values and guiding principles. Principles are general laws and truths, or a personal or specific basis of conduct and management. Do you run your life under a set of principles that guide you? If not, then what is at the core of your decisions? Let's say a guiding principle was 'do no harm onto others'. To live an authentic principle-based life, this would have to be demonstrated in everything you do and everything you stand for. Values are not too dissimilar. Values are individual beliefs that motivate people and the set of principles that help you decide what to do. Values are fascinating. First, you don't choose your values, they choose you. But once you identify your values, the only way to live in congruence with them is blanket application, not partial application. For example, you can't say, 'I believe in diversity and inclusion of thinking [but not in this instance because it's not what I think],' or, 'I believe in equity in the workplace [but not in this instance because they're not the same as me],' or, 'I believe everyone should be fairly paid [but only under my conditions].' Selecting where and when to apply your values doesn't make you virtuous, it makes you a walking contradiction and chameleon that only believes in a truth that you're making up as you go. When you are clear on your values and principles, making good judgement calls has a sound basis. That's why working for a value-aligned organisation is imperative. Let's say equity was one of your core values, but the value of the organisation was profit first, people second. You are aware that the budgets were already undercooked, and now your manager wants you to go in hard and negotiate more off the tender sum. You know very well that this puts the contractor at high risk of losing money. What will you do? Be clear and steadfast in your value and principles no matter what comes your way, and you will set out a track record of integrity for yourself that few can claim to have all the same.

'Depend upon yourself. Make your judgement trustworthy
by trusting it. You can develop good judgement as you do the
muscles of your body – by judicious, daily exercise. To be known
as a man of sound judgement will be much in your favour.'
– Grantland Rice

Of equal importance to making great judgement calls is knowing when to not make a call. Have you ever been triggered by a
friend that you just snap, only to think later on, *I shouldn't have*
said that? Or when you were so sleep deprived that you just suf-
ficed to eating fast food which was a great idea only at the time?
It's important to identify your states of being that aren't conducive
to you making good judgement calls. I know my triggers well,
and during those times it's best I disengage with others. One is
when my energy feels irritated, I know I need to be alone, and my
energy is too low to make a judgement, so I purposely don't make
it then. If you're frustrated at work, stressed out, burntout, then
you're not in an optimal state to make a call. At the same time,
you do need to learn how to make good judgement calls despite
your own emotional state. Exercising control over your emotional
disposition and learning how to observe your emotions, and not
becoming your emotions, is key to learning how to perform well
in high-pressure situations. Never base your judgements on how
you feel because feelings change. Think of it this way: if a manager
is angry, you wouldn't want them making key decisions on your
pay and promotion, especially if they can't separate the two factors.
Nor should anyone go out and buy a car simply because they're in a
happy mood. Separating judgement calls from your emotions and
the states in which you shouldn't make judgements will put you in

a category above the rest. You're getting paid by your employer to constantly make really sound judgements with positive long-term impacts for the organisation. This will also work to build trust in you over a long period of time, and you may just find people coming to you asking you for your perspective on a situation.

TRIGGER QUESTIONS

1. When was the last time you exercised great judgement?
2. Where do your morality and ethics come from? How do you form your principles and values?
3. Do you only make great judgement calls that suit your intentions?
4. Are you aware of your own personal biases, motivations and unconscious preferences?
5. What are your core values? Have you been making decisions in alignment with them?
6. Are there people in your life who have consistently made great judgements for themselves? What results do they have today in comparison to those who haven't?

YOUNG GUN BULLETS

- Identify the next big call that needs to be made on a project. Ask if you can observe the decision-making process to identify the inputs for consideration and how said decision-makers have concluded.

- Make a set of rules for quick decisions, i.e. every day you read ten pages or you only check emails twice a day. Remaking a decision instead of abiding by your own rules creates decision fatigue and gives you too many mental concessions. Automate and repeat routine decisions to free your mind for more weighted considerations.
- Consider all opposing viewpoints from stakeholders prior to coming to a decision. When you are gathering this, listen to understand and not to respond.

K

KNOWLEDGE

NŎL'ĬJ

THE SUM OR RANGE OF WHAT HAS BEEN
PERCEIVED, DISCOVERED OR LEARNED

---

*'The greatest enemy of knowledge is not ignorance; it is the
illusion of knowledge.' – Daniel J Boorstin*

American writer, futurist and businessman Alvin Toffler said,
'The illiterate of the twenty-first century will not be those who
cannot read and write, but those who cannot learn, unlearn and
relearn.' We're in a day and age when the speed of information
and insight is rapidly produced and disseminated. There was no
other point in time, other than the internet age, where we have
the body of knowledge generated by human history available to
us. And per microsecond, more and more is generated. Markets
change fast, new skills emerge and those that were once revered

are rendered low value. Truly having success in today's age is premised on staying relevant. Most people rely on their relevancy from a degree they did in 1999 which was based on teachings from 1986. Imagine if doctors took the same approach as most professionals. Would you want to be treated by a doctor who last updated their knowledge base when they graduated? I wouldn't think so. Your learning doesn't stop with your degree, it's where it begins. Knowledge isn't only about what you already know, but the speed at which you can expand your knowledge base and adapting it to what's relevant and pressing now, so you can be in the best position possible to respond and maximise opportunity.

There is the technical proficiency that you are developing at work, but over and above that, having a macro view of what is happening in the construction industry is imperative to your knowledge base too. Engaging with industry-specific content – such as podcasts, magazines, blogs, articles, white papers, conferences and events – is imperative to your knowledge of the industry. Constant engagement and keeping their finger on the pulse is a recurring trait in the exemplary leaders and industry titans I interview for my podcast. You can always measure a person's interest in what they do if they'll do it without force. During university, deadlines and submissions forced you to research. Can you do it now without any reprieve or reward? And I do this daily as well, for I am, after all, in the business of thinking. The thing with knowledge is that no-one can take it away from you, and if you consistently do this for years, you will have placed such a major gap between you and those around you, by sheer virtue of what you know. And you'll find that most people aren't prepared to do this on a consistent basis, because they're not curious, they're satisfied. Develop your expertise so that you will be able to make a valuable contribution to any conversation related to your field or niche that you find yourself in.

> ## YOUNG GUN PRINCIPLE
> Consistently and consciously expand your field of knowledge and expertise in your area in order to gain a competitive edge.

As has been mentioned beforehand, most people will teach you what to think, not how to think. There is one paradigm of thinking when it comes to expanding your knowledge that will give you the greatest compounding advantage. That is to think like an entrepreneur, which is opposite to thinking like an employee. You don't need to become an entrepreneur, but you certainly need to think like one. Having an enterprising mind will allow you to create and see opportunities where others aren't even looking, or even know that they need to look in that direction. By sheer virtue of thinking like an entrepreneur, you will find that drive to want to increase your knowledge base instead of having such a myopic world view. When you start to see the world through an entrepreneurial lens, you will quickly see how much you don't know to be successful in any creative venture. A key marker of entrepreneurial thinking is creativity. What do you really know of being creative? When was the last time you created something out of nothing from your own imagination? Do you know that imagination is the most powerful faculty of your mind but the least used? As you seek to expand your thinking, you will also seek to expand the knowledge to support your new thoughts (or so does a true young gun). To be an entrepreneurial thinker first requires creativity in your cognition. Start asking more questions and articulating more thoughts with, *What if we did this* ... and see where the conversation goes. You may have heard the old adage 'creativity is the mother of invention'. Sometimes in corporate, employees are expected to generate solutions quick, there's not much that can linger or stay open. This reduces the ability to sit in the discomfort of not knowing. A slight paradox – we get to a state of knowing through being able to sit in prolonged periods of not knowing. 'The only true wisdom is in knowing you know nothing,' said Socrates. To think like an entrepreneur is not to rush to a conclusion.

Another characteristic of entrepreneurial thinking is to be open to failing, trying, tweaking and doing that all over again with no promised outcomes. This is where more people get deterred and consider it a failure, only to not realise that iteration is simply part of the process. The first edit of my book was not the one that got published. Experimentation is an essential factor to creativity, which instils an ability to learn from failure and go again. It's not even a failure, it's just a lesson. There is no single person who has success, by global definitions, that got to where they are by giving up after one go. It's not talent that wins the race, it's tenacity and the ambition to keep on going in the face of all setbacks. The path to success may feel crowded at the bottom but it becomes significantly less competitive the more you edge towards the top. And a key part of an entrepreneurial mindset is to see possibilities not impossibilities. When someone immediately says, 'That won't work,' they have demonstrated how closed-minded they are. When I started The Construction Coach, I didn't look in the rear-view mirror to see if it's been done before. I did look into the future to see what could be possible, and that's what made it happen. You will find opportunities that are there, ready for the taking, if you start to think like an entrepreneur and not an employee. Your body of knowledge will become significantly expansive if you adopt this line of thinking.

'We are drowning in information but starved for knowledge.'
– John Naisbitt

The greatest feedback loop I have as a mentor is when clients come to me with wins. I am always deeply humbled when they attribute their success to me, or due to my involvement. What I always get them to do immediately is recognise that it was them. They had it in them, I am their guide, providing them with the pathway, frameworks and tools to achieve what they want. I then get them to reflect on what *they* did really well with what they were given to achieve their goals, so that they can do it again. You already have a significant amount of knowledge within you, but the lessons may not have been extracted. That's why I get my clients to pause, contemplate and reflect on what they did. Learning to sit back, clear your mind and make space for deep contemplation on all your moves will unlock a body of knowledge that no theory can ever impress onto you. Most people live mechanically and on autopilot, never truly stopping to reflect. Experiences only matter when they are evaluated and you extract the lesson. Otherwise, you will find yourself repeating the same experiences over and over again until you learn the lesson, which puts a severe cap on your knowledge.

TRIGGER QUESTIONS

1. Do you have a balanced left brain (logical and analytical) and right brain (creative and imaginative) approach to your career and life?
2. Would you feel comfortable going to a networking event and striking up conversation with anyone?
3. Do you have limited views about attaining knowledge and expertise – such as, it's only possible through conventional education? How are these views holding you back?
4. Are you someone who is driven to know a little about a lot or a lot about little?
5. Can you tell the difference between information and knowledge? What is the difference?
6. Do you act consistently with your knowledge?

YOUNG GUN BULLETS

- Spend ten to twenty minutes a day for the next 365 days consuming industry-relevant knowledge through accredited sources in any medium.
- Come up with one new, novel and creative idea per month that would improve an area of your role or organisation. Discuss it with your team and identify if any can be implemented.
- Enrol yourself in a coaching or mentoring program of your own accord and choosing within the next six months to build your mindset and skillset.

L

LIABILITY

LĪ″ə-BĬL′Ĭ-TĒ

SOMETHING FOR WHICH ONE IS LIABLE; AN
OBLIGATION, RESPONSIBILITY OR DEBT

'Extreme ownership is a mindset, an attitude.'
– Jocko Willink

The antithesis of taking liability for your own actions falls under
the colloquialism of 'throwing someone under the bus'. As I have
been there under the proverbial bus, it's extremely unpleasant
to have someone shift all the blame when they were equal parts
involved in the outcome. Extreme ownership is assuming full
liability for all that happens within your sphere of influence.
It's a universal principle I have covered in my other two books,
and because of its importance to your commitment to higher
standards and excellence, it needs to be covered again. When

you have been given a responsibility, a task or are involved in a certain function on a project, you need to take full liability for the outcomes of it. It's on you. It's very easy to always pass the blame onto another party – the consultant didn't respond, the subcontractor couldn't submit their price, the head contractor won't provide all the information. Now, these may all be legitimate reasons, but regardless of what the other party says or does, you are still liable for the intended outcome. Those around you will be looking to understand how you are actively taking responsibility for delivery of the outcome they tasked you with. One of my constructors once called me in a flurry regarding a perceived error at work. She misunderstood the prioritisation of tasks and didn't get tower crane pricing in time for the tender close. This was the first submission of the tender, and there was a rated allowance for tower cranes, but she didn't know that. Her plan was to first speak to the subcontractor and explain the situation and got a firm date for when a quote will be received. She then fronted the estimating manager who wasn't concerned but impressed at her initiative and honesty and how professionally she dealt with the problem by already having a solution in place. It's not that you're expected to know it all, but you are expected to do all you can in your power and ability to deliver and rectify the situation.

YOUNG GUN PRINCIPLE

Assume full liability and responsibility for your work and
life outcomes to demonstrate your character and integrity
within your team and avoid shifting the blame to others.

Assuming full liability for your work certainly doesn't mean that you will know all you need to do along the way, which is where asking questions (see Q for Questions) is imperative. You certainly aren't expected to know it all, but you are expected to approach people within your team to find out. The onus is also on the management team to ensure that proper instruction and information has been made available so a graduate can proceed with the task. In taking full liability, you are also demonstrating a high level of accountability. I have worked with subpar management who weren't able to see the errors in their own ways and weren't willing to show accountability. This diminishes the respect that you earn within a workplace. To avoid becoming a manager that doesn't stand up for or support their team, get into the mindset from day one of accountability over your actions. It requires honesty in your character to own up to your errors and give a transparent account of where things may have gone wrong. As fear-inducing as this may be for a young gun, it's also part of your character development, and if you're working with a supportive team who understand the value of mistakes, assuredly you won't be berated for it.

'If a person has an ego, he will never blame himself in his life for anything, instead he will blame others for his own mistake.'
— Jocko Willink

You will also get to the stage of your career when you'll have a graduate working under you, and for their learning and outcomes, you are also liable. You never throw a graduate, or anyone for that matter, under the bus – remember, you were one not so long ago. You'll gain their trust, respect and best work ethic when you also show liability for their outcomes. If a graduate that worked under me made a mistake, I will always front up to them that it was on me to explain it to them in a way that made sense to them. You will come across many scenarios, whether upstream or downstream, that will require you to assume liability, and it's in your best long-term interest to always do so.

Finally, you have a decision to make. Are you going to spend more time making your goals come into fruition or spend more time with your orchestra of excuses? The thing with excuses is that you can hang around them until the end of time. However, opportunity of any nature has a limited window to capture it. It's incredible how when most people are faced with any sort of opportunity – from joining a mentoring program to switching positions – they will have a barrage of excuses, from 'it's not the right time' to 'I'm not ready' and so on. If you are constantly waiting for perfect conditions in order to do anything new or worthwhile, you'll be waiting forever. There is no such thing as the perfect time. Successful people talk themselves into making decisions that are good for them. Unsuccessful people talk themselves out of making decisions, and then typically seek validation from equally unsuccessful people that they made the right decision. Are you really going to construct your whole career and life off a foundation of excuses? Will that not crumble and fall? You truly need to reflect, for how much longer can you put off what you need to do, which is investing in yourself, however that may look right now. There is a cost to inaction and inactivity. Using a mentoring program, for example. Some may think that today they saved $5,000. However, they haven't quantified the cost of missed opportunities, the cost of compounding effects of their knowledge and also the intangible benefits that come with mentoring. Let's take saying yes to a new and more senior opportunity. If someone thinks they're not ready, they're missing out on the fiscal benefit, but also the opportunity to learn and diversify their skills and experiences. A decision made in comfort today will 100% yield uncomfortable outcomes in the medium- to long-term. So, if you choose comfort over growth, you will recede into the background of mediocrity and achieve extremely low levels of sporadic success.

TRIGGER QUESTIONS

1. When something doesn't go your way, do you tend to immediately seek to blame and pass responsibility?
2. How would your life change if you took 100% responsibility over everything that happened?
3. Do you think you will be more or less empowered if you lived by the extreme ownership principle?
4. In what areas of your life can you take more ownership for the results that you have?
5. Have you been believing your excuses to validate staying in your comfort zone? Make a list of all the missed opportunities because of this. Do you think this is a suitable approach in the face of your ambitions and goals?
6. Do you hold yourself accountable and to high standards on a regular basis, even if it's not convenient to you?

YOUNG GUN BULLETS

- For the next thirty days, take on full responsibility for everything that is happening in your life, whether you feel it was your doing or not. Reflect after thirty days if you felt more in control or less.
- For the next thirty days, eliminate all excuses and complaints from your conversation with yourself. Make it a hard and fast rule for yourself and consider a form of pain if you break it. For example, each time you make an excuse, you must give $50 to charity.
- Follow through on 100% of the things you say you will do in the time frame specified by not allowing yourself to procrastinate. Reflect on how your productivity and outputs have significantly improved.

M

MEETINGS

MĒ'TĬNG

THE ACT OR PROCESS OR AN INSTANCE OF COMING
TOGETHER; AN ENCOUNTER

---

*'When the outcome of a meeting is to have another meeting,
it has been a lousy meeting.' – Herbert Hoover*

You weren't born to sit in meetings, alas, here you are. It's an activity that fills up the working week, the bane of professionals' existence, and the cause of much unproductiveness. Yet the calendars are full and 'back-to-back' with meetings. Just ask someone you work with if they think they'll be able to get more done and work less hours if they had less (useless) meetings. According to research by Zippia, organisations spend roughly 15% of their time on meetings, with surveys showing that 71% of those meetings are considered unproductive. An estimated $37 billion is lost per year to unproductive meetings. Twenty-four billion hours are wasted each year as the result of unproductive meetings and the average corporate employee spends four hours preparing for and attending meetings per week. Above the fiscal implication, there's the emotional implication of excessive meetings, including stress, burn-out, disengagement and loss of productivity. *MIT Sloan Management Review* have even conducted research into the loss of meeting productivity to detail a condition called 'meeting recovery syndrome', in which attendees lose time reeling as they mentally recover from a bad meeting. It's not just the after-effect. The average mind will give itself a concession in anticipation of an upcoming meeting, as to not start a task because of an upcoming interruption. The percentages and statistics are endless as to the abyss of time and money that meetings are. Yet, there is no training or effort to make workplace gatherings more efficient or even challenge how they happen. With an increase in flexible and remote working, there is a need to revisit the bane of corporate personnel's existence. To become more effective and efficient and to stand out from the lax approach and time-wasting activities, a young gun needs to be sharper in their approach to and in meetings.

First, let us establish a few meeting ground rules. It shouldn't be a given that all meetings need to be half an hour or an hour. Just because the Outlook calendar automatically splits its calendar as such doesn't mean you have to. Meetings can be scheduled for fifteen minutes, twenty minutes, forty-five minutes. I know this sounds simple, but the first time I scheduled in a twenty-minute meeting, I immediately got asked why I did that. If you schedule in a meeting for twenty minutes, you are immediately narrowing the opportunity to ramble on. It's imperative that meetings start and end on the scheduled time, out of respect for your own time and that of others. Of equal importance is to ascertain first if there is a requirement for a meeting. Meetings should not be held purely for the purpose of sharing information, that can be done through other mediums. Meetings should be used to provide outcome-based discussions, provide clarity on an issue and create forward momentum, and also facilitate decision-making, and should only happen in real-time if it cannot be achieved through other mediums first. If people leave a meeting unclear on what to do, then it was a waste of time. Meetings also shouldn't have excessive people in attendance. Think of the 'two-pizza rule' by Jeff Bezos, founder of Amazon. If two pizzas cannot feed a meeting, then you have too many people at the meeting. The participants in attendance should be the ones who can make a meaningful contribution. At first, to aid your learning, I do encourage you to tag along to meetings as this is where you will gain project insight and create an avenue to form relationships. However, don't get caught up in the false facade of meetings equalling productivity.

YOUNG GUN PRINCIPLE

Don't let excessive, elongated meetings override your time. Introduce improved meeting habits into the workplace to create effectiveness and increased productiveness in your own work and time management.

Now onto the actual meeting conduct. If a person is not engaged within the meeting, they shouldn't have to be there and can catch up on the outcome later. Founder of Tesla and Space X, Elon Musk, has a stark approach to this; 'Walk out of a meeting or drop off a call as soon as it is obvious you aren't adding value.' Of course, if this isn't accepted practice you will be reprimanded, but keep this in mind as you seek to determine what meetings you should be at and who should further be in attendance. Presenteeism for the sake of it at meetings is a massive time and resource drain. When a meeting invitation is sent out, ensure it's with an agenda. This can be a few bullet points as to what needs to be covered. The agenda will also allow people to prepare accordingly. Further time is leaked in meetings when people don't come prepared and will have to get back to you. If you are invited to a meeting and there is no agenda, have confidence to ask for one, so you can equally prepare accordingly and have the information you need at hand. Again, the focus of meetings should be for resolve and results. As the young gun, you may not be the one generating the result because of technical knowledge or other constraints, but you can certainly push for one. More likely than not, your duty in meetings will be to take meeting minutes. I don't know what's worse, the number of meetings or the administration of recording them. There are multiple co-working platforms, ways to record actions over and above a graduate taking minutes, sending them for review, sending them out, only for no-one to action anything and go to the next meeting to simply update the due date. When you are taking minutes, you may not know everything that is being discussed. In this instance, just scribe down verbatim and create minutes after. I would recommend typing and not handwriting which eliminates a duplication of effort. If you are familiar with the meeting minutes and content discussed, then update the meeting minutes live. If it needs to be internally reviewed, send it for review straight away. Meeting minutes need to go out twenty-four to forty-eight hours from the meeting. I haven't met a graduate who enjoys doing this, but the quicker they move along to participants, the better. Even if there are no formal meeting minutes, take notes and send them out to all participants. There should always be a record of the discussion. As a young gun, ensure that you are asking sufficient questions during a meeting, as meetings and discussions will be your key learning grounds (if you actively participate). You will also be positioned as an important meeting attendee by driving discussion and keeping all participants engaged. Most juniors in a meeting will refrain from speaking as to avoid being perceived as inept, but the only way to overcome this is by asking questions and contributing. Ensure that when the agenda of the meeting has been concluded, the meeting finishes and the action items and follow-up dates are clearly established. You should also think creatively as to how meetings can be held – could you have a standing fifteen-minute catch-up, a lunch and meet, or if someone is walking to a destination onsite, can you join them for a discussion. A meeting doesn't have to be a conventional sit-down one.

'Meetings are indispensable when you don't want to do anything.' – John Kenneth Galbraith

With the introduction of working from home and remote work due to events of recent times, online meetings are a new arena that many have had to navigate. All the above is equally applicable for meetings, but also consider if the timing of the meeting for the person working at home suits. If they have children, early morning may not suit. Notify people in advance that videos must be on (or if this is an audio-only call). When cameras are on, people will be more likely to be engaged and avoid distractions. Video is imperative to facilitate connection and generate the sense of being in a room together. There can be overuse of virtual meetings when people are working remotely to generate the sense of connectedness, and meeting fatigue can set in. Do truly consider if the meeting could have been an email.

To conclude, ensure that you are present and focused within the meeting, and that especially as a junior, you won't know all that is being discussed, but you are there to learn. Asking brilliant questions and facilitating engagement is an important function of the meeting and will enable you to position yourself well within the project team when you can demonstrate the skill to run results-orientated, sharp and focused meetings.

TRIGGER QUESTIONS

1. Is your time at work overly controlled by useless meetings? Is there a process at work for calling meetings?
2. Are you wasting time before and after meetings? If yes, how can you cut down the lag time around meetings?
3. Are there existing meetings at work you can take more ownership over to ensure the efforts are more productive?
4. Do you feel that meeting goals and agendas are being achieved? If not, where are the leaks and inefficiencies occurring?
5. What is currently working in meetings? What isn't and needs to stop?

6. Do you consider yourself to be a proactive participant in meetings? If not, what do you need to be doing to attain more benefit from attending meetings?

YOUNG GUN BULLETS

- Create a framework for assessment whether a meeting is required. Share this with your team for feedback and explain why controlling meeting time is imperative.
- If you are part of a meeting, ask if you can chair it to ensure that the agenda is covered on time. Issue meeting minutes and actions within forty-eight hours of the meeting occurrence and set a time to follow up actions to ensure the meeting wasn't a moot exercise.
- Set strict time blocks during your work week as to when you will have meetings and when you will allocate time for deep work.

N

NETWORKS

NĚT'WÛRK"

AN EXTENDED GROUP OF PEOPLE WITH SIMILAR
INTERESTS OR CONCERNS WHO INTERACT AND
REMAIN IN INFORMAL CONTACT FOR MUTUAL
ASSISTANCE OR SUPPORT

'Networking is not about just connecting people. It's about connecting people with people, people with ideas, and people with opportunities.' – Michele Jennae

Most graduates will invest a fleeting yet intense period of effort to build their networks post-graduation to attain employment. Most fail to realise that networking will be one of the keys to them attaining employment and it would have been more beneficial to nurture a network three years ago, not three years later. And then, once they're employed, most, if not all, efforts to sustain the connections are gone with the main goal being attained. There is certainly an adjustment period between the anarchy that ruled a job-seeker's schedule to that of a professional, but that intensity of the transitional phase doesn't last forever. And then months or years down the line, a graduate (now with experience) finds themselves in the same position of requiring or wanting an alternative opportunity. But again, have been caught out with no network, as their efforts were lax, thinking one opportunity will suffice forever, and they have to again take the hunting approach to finding opportunity instead of being head-hunted. The key to a network is to build and nurture it when you don't need it, so it can be ready for toiling when you do need it. It aligns with the old adage 'the same day you plant the seed is not the day you eat the fruit'. You will continually find yourself in the dark of the industry if you don't take a proactive and consistent approach to constructing your networks. As some may learn the hard way, the construction industry is so intricately connected and there are little degrees of separation between people. Not being part of the fold means not developing your relationship equity.

A cornerstone of the construction industry is who you know and who knows you, and the one type of equity that will take you the furthest is relationship equity. I spent seven years constructing the networks, via facilitating connections, adding value, volunteering and showing up to events. In 2017, I went to circa twenty-seven networking events. Did I want something immediately? No. Did I have an immediate need that needed to be fulfilled? Also no. Networking isn't about me, it's what I can do for others. And it's the consistency in my approach that built the runway for all that I do today. It's because of my networks that I was able to unlock doors and access opportunities that wouldn't have been available if it wasn't via a connection. I was able to eventually ask for return value, because I'd demonstrated consistent value and effort without expecting anything in return. If you will only do things because there is an immediate reward, you're already setting yourself up for failure. As a young gun, the focus on relationships can be lost, with the immediacy of wanting to do so well technically and to be an exceptional performer in your role. This should never bar you from expanding your networks offline and online. Because as you move up the career hierarchy, the opportunities that you're looking for will become more exclusive, and they're rarely, if ever, advertised. Without a network, you won't be able to leverage or scale your career as effectively as the person who can make one or two calls to open the right doors or call in a timely favour.

> ## YOUNG GUN PRINCIPLE
> Your relationship equity and what goes into your favour bank is invaluable to your progression and exposure to opportunities, which is why constructing your networks should always be a high priority.

How do you truly think promotions for senior positions or business partnerships happen in the industry? Through networks, of course. There are ample examples of unique opportunities that came through networks on my podcast, *Constructing You*. Many guests have detailed that one call where they were tapped on the shoulder for a CEO position, next great project, new partnership. They rarely, if ever, took the conventional approach of hunting for it. They were head-hunted. They, and only they, got the call. People would much rather do business with people that they know and trust. As a young gun, it can be intimidating to talk to the seniors within an organisation, or seniors in the industry generally. If you have your eye on a senior position, the iconic project, the dream company, then you need to build leverage, influence and connections today. When you are seeking to facilitate a human-to-human connection, experience matters not, only curiosity in the first instance. Make the conscious effort to at least get to know the people of influence in the business and/or industry. Instigate the conversation at the least, and you can do this by walking up to them if they're seemingly free or sending an email request for a fifteen-minute conversation. There is no shortage of ways in which you can get on their radar. The onus is on you to raise your hand and demonstrate your presence and promote yourself upstream. Assuredly, few management staff will go out of their way to promote you or your best interests (and if they do, thank them, they're a rare find). Don't be averse to also posting your achievements, passions and projects on social media platforms. I would be at a work function or meeting, and they would mention in conversation something they saw online that I posted. There are many benefits of maintaining a social media presence, which is outside the scope of this book, but the aforementioned would be one. Especially if you are a young gun based onsite, you need to find ways to engage with management within the office. People will also hire, fire and promote based on those within their immediate proximity, so don't underestimate the advantage of long-term rapport-building.

'The currency of real networking is not greed but generosity.'
– Keith Ferrazzi

Relationship-building is to equally extend to subcontractors. There is a negative side to the industry which is to 'screw down' the subcontractors' pricing to meet budgets. This is a core issue in the industry, as there are too many players in the marketplace, meaning clients have choice. When most clients are cost-centric not value-centric, they'll be seeking the lowest bid. The clients are the root cause of this mentality, the rest of the industry just enforces it. A client should always pay what is fair and reasonable, but I'm sure it wasn't the first time that what seemed to be the lowest bid at the outset ended up being the highest. To meet the initial near-impossible budget, the cost cutting gets pushed downstream. There are times when a subcontractor will expect a negotiation, and there are times when it's not suitable. If you constantly screw down the subcontractor, you will be left high and dry in hours of need when you really need them to come through. If you haven't taken a fair and reasonable approach during a project with a contractor (head or sub), you don't have the right to call in a favour or ask them to do something pro-bono. Do not discount subcontractors as key players in your professional network, for they are the ones doing the building construction, after all. It's through the cycle of goodwill and a perspective of mutually beneficial outcomes that contractors (who will forever be my favourite) have saved me against critical outcomes and decisive moments onsite. When I worked at Melbourne Airport, we had the DDA consultant (disability access) assess that a ramp was off-grade and wouldn't pass for practical completion (PC) which was days away. Within days, we had to jackhammer out the concrete and repour it. But the handrail also needed to be remade, as the existing one would be noncompliant against the new ramp. It can typically take ten days to see a new handrail onsite, but I had it there in three, and managed to get DDA sign-off. Mind you, this was all done in December, which in the lead up to Christmas, can be a stretch to achieve. Five years later, and I still remember that handrail and how many phone calls were made to get it. As simple as it may sound, if there was no handrail, there was no PC. It was the nurtured relationship with the subcontractors that allowed us to band together and come through. They didn't want to let anyone down and neither did I. A contractor who gets beat around won't make magic happen or won't do it without significant penalty. Treat your contractors with respect, for at the end of the day, they're the ones building our buildings.

Finally, comes the importance of stakeholder management. It can sometimes feel that all we really do is go through a cycle of managing each other's expectations and delivering on outcomes. If that's not what people do for work, then what do they do? Stakeholder management is, fundamentally, expectation management. When you say you will get back to someone by Friday with a resolution, for example, they have that expectation. If Friday comes and goes and they hear back from you two weeks later, they have defined a perception about you which may or may not be true. If you said you will get back to someone by Friday, and you are not able to do so, then you need to update the expectation as to when you will realistically do that. It's the same with a tender. If a contractor is expecting to hear back by a certain date, extend the courtesy, even if it's to say that you have no new information or further updates. If you say A and do B, you aren't acting with integrity on your word and failing on the expectations that were set. Transparency is pivotal to this, as you will find most people are understanding if you approach an explanation with honesty instead of going silent. Like you, most don't like being left in the dark or suspended in motion. You can never over-communicate, which is a stronger approach than under-communicating. If you are consistent in simply doing what you say, you will build a trackrecord that will be hard to fault.

TRIGGER QUESTIONS

1. Do you see the long-term benefit of building your network?
2. Are you consciously building your network now when you don't need it, ready for when you do?
3. Do you have patience to sow the seeds and wait to reap the harvest of your network?
4. How do you maintain and nurture the connections you have already made?
5. Are you letting the fear of networking prevent you from meeting people instead of building the skillset to do so?
6. How can you become a connector in your network to add more value to your existing connections?

YOUNG GUN BULLETS

- Identify associations or groups that hosts events you are interested in building a network with and potentially contribute to. Set a goal to go to all upcoming events in the next twelve months that align with your interests and have opportunity for you to meet people.
- Suggest an internal networking event or boardroom lunch with a focus topic (lunch and learn) to create networking opportunities within the organisation with people that you wouldn't usually talk to. You could also organise a team lunch or after-work drinks event.
- Look for committees you can join that align with the value you seek to create in the industry and apply for a position. You will rapidly broaden your networks through these quasi-professional settings and have an opportunity to connect and work with people you wouldn't have access to come your day job.

O

ORGANISATION

ÔR″Gə-Nĭ-ZĀ′SHƏN

A MANNER OF ACCOMPLISHING SOMETHING IN AN
ORDERLY OR EFFICIENT WAY

---

*'Organising is what you do before you do something, so that
when you do it, it is not all mixed up.'* – A. A. Milne

There's a temporary sense of overwhelm as young guns enter the
industry with the sudden volume of work that needs to be done
– daily. A productive balance of effectiveness and efficiency will
allow for optimal organisation, which will enhance productivity, reduce unnecessary stress and allow you to leave work at
a reasonable time. Organisation and prioritisation go hand in
hand, but to be organised, one must first know their priorities.
When I worked on a large project that had satellite projects
run with different teams, prioritisation became a pressing issue.

What was a priority to one project manager conflicted with the priority of another project manager, and the frustration built up quick within all subordinates, who were constantly being reactive as the goalposts moved. Not everything is a priority, and this needs to be assessed on what would be the consequence if it wasn't delivered by the expected due date. Naturally, with the pressures from just about every stakeholder, it can seem that everything is a priority, but it isn't. What I used to do on project delivery was first make a master list of all the tasks that needed to be done every Monday morning. This would include new tasks and any carry-over tasks from the previous week. Then I would make a daily sub-list, as to which of those items I would focus on that week. There had to be time to allocate to ongoing work, such as cost control and tendering, meetings, and then ancillary issues which would arise. I would then check back at the end of the day and check what I have achieved, and then plan the next day before I would leave work. But even within the list of tasks for the day, it can be tempting to engage with the 'low-hanging fruit' type of tasks, which only give a false sense of momentum. Ensure that within your daily lists, you have a clear sense as to what needs to be addressed first. Don't leave the most important tasks to the end of the day. To ascertain priorities from your lists, assess them per the Eisenhower Matrix. Former US president Dwight Eisenhower developed the matrix, which is a simple four-quadrant box to assign different statuses to tasks, separating 'urgent' tasks from 'important' ones. When looking at how to prioritise tasks best, allocate them under one of the following:

- **Urgent and important:** Do these tasks as soon as possible.

- **Important, but not urgent:** Decide when you'll do these and schedule it.

- **Urgent, but not important:** Delegate these tasks to someone else or do it when you have spare time.

- **Neither urgent nor important:** Drop these from your schedule as soon as possible.

YOUNG GUN PRINCIPLE

Ensure that you are doing the critical work first and when you are most alert and present. Don't leave important tasks to the end of the day.

To get organised now that you have your priorities, I want to share a few key hacks that allowed me to control most of my time at work. There is a plethora of productivity hacks available for you to explore, but I will only list those that I've tried and tested.

1. Turn off email notifications. Notifications generally work to provide dopamine hits to your mind, making them addictive. There is a false sense that with each notification that arises, you must respond immediately. You don't. Turn off your Outlook email notifications, so when you are working on your computer, you aren't constantly distracted by pop-ups. The same goes for your phone. If an email is so urgent, it should probably have been a phone call. This also sets the expectations of those dealing with you that if they want you to see something immediately, it begs a phone call. Only check emails a maximum of two or three times a day and use

your least productive hours (usually there's a lull around 3pm for most people) to respond to emails. If you start responding immediately, people will also start expecting immediate responses from you. When you are constantly reactive, and a slave to your inbox, you are always dealing with others' priorities and not your own.

2. Answer the phone when you can, not when it rings. Like all other tasks, taking phone calls and responding to calls has dedicated windows to do so. I know this will be unpopular advice. When I worked as a contract administrator, I'd be generating the monthly cost reports. This would take a few blocks of time in the weeks leading to submission to generate it and required a deep level of concentration. And then I would answer the phone, get derailed from what I was doing, and before I knew it, hours had gone by. Of course, if you are expecting an urgent call or there are important activities that need you to be present at, then answer. But if you are engaged in your own priority work, don't take the phone call. Call the person back. Or, if you must, find out what it's about and advise when you will call them back. You need to protect the time you have dedicated to undertaking the priority and meaningful work, instead of constantly responding to the lights and sounds of your phone. What tends to happen is that when the phone is unlocked after a phone call, most people will be sucked into it, checking the socials and emails, and wasting more time. My phone was always on vibrate during work hours, as it works to remove the distraction and reduce the urge to constantly check my phone.

3. Avoid multitasking. Few people have a truly flexible and

agile mind where they can switch gears with ease without losing focus or productivity. For the rest of us, multitasking is a myth. Our brains are only wired to do one thing at a time, and if you think you can multitask, ask yourself if you are doing an average job on two things instead of a brilliant job on one thing? It's a fault in professionals' thinking that this generates productivity, but it only results in half efforts applied here and there. You are going to get more momentum by intense periods of focus than not.

4. Use tools that suit you. I love pen and paper to capture my activities, and I'll colour code it all the same. You can use Outlook, Trello and the like to organise, list and time-block your day. Use whatever works for you to note and control deadlines, key tasks and priorities.

5. Have an organised desk. When I worked onsite, I avoided printing as much as possible. Not just that I saw it as a waste, but every sheet of paper then duplicates the effort in filing, considering what to do with it or throwing it away. So I frequently had a pretty empty desk, which created the feeling of order. If you are a hoarder, then use this system. Every time you pick up a piece of paper or a document on your desk, put a dot on it. If a document has three dots and you still haven't done anything with it, you don't need it; throw it away. The same works for your desktop.

6. Don't spend time organising your email inbox into many folders. Outlook has a search function for that reason, so you can find what you need. If you pay attention, you probably use this anyway without manually looking for the email. Keep your folders simple, by having a folder with 'to action'

emails and then 'closed'. This keeps your main inbox at zero for most of the time, but also saves you the unnecessary time of filing.

7. Organise your time around when you know you work best. If you are a morning person, avoid scheduling meetings during your prime time. Schedule it for later in the day, where possible. If you get your best work done in the afternoon, then vice versa. You want to optimise your day around your effectiveness, so you can get the most done. And when you have a schedule in place, stick to it. There's no point in having the best laid-out plans if they aren't to be followed. You're better off working in bursts, so ensure that you take a few minutes break to get up and remove yourself from the screen. Whilst it seems counterintuitive to stop working, it will replenish your energy and refresh the mind, allowing you to get more focused and meaningful work completed.

'The secret of all victory lies in the organisation of the non-obvious.' – Oswald Spengler

As a relative junior onsite, you will also be called upon to do menial tasks, outstanding but not urgent tasks that others haven't gotten around to completing. Filing and labelling being the most common. There's a saying in corporate, that 'sh*t flows downhill'. Meaning, you'll be tasked with the roles that have been pending and outstanding for quite some time, that management have been waiting to pass onto someone downstream. No-one really likes doing them, but it won't be management doing them. It's simply not worth their hourly rate. You will, in the short-term, need to take this in your stride and do the less than average jobs. The only consideration is that if the task does fall under someone else's core function, you shouldn't be doing their work for them so they can leave early. When you are starting off, you won't get to immediately work on the major packages, tough contract negotiations or run client meetings. That will come with experience and demonstration of capability. When you do get tasked with menial work, ensure that you give clear expectation to the assignee as to how much time you can dedicate to it given your other priorities. If it is to take your focus, then agree on a timeframe for completing the task. Remember, this too shall pass. Your attitude to getting done the insignificant will be a determining factor as to how much significant work you'll be tasked with.

As a young gun, your diligence and effort will be rewarded with more work. At times, you will be tasked with competing priorities, because the superiors should want you on their team, of course. Management can sometimes forget how long a task takes as a graduate when you are both learning and doing at the same time. From the perspective of each manager, their tasks are just as important as the other, and there are limits at times as to how many tasks you can undertake at the same time. When this situation arises, you need to be the manager in this situation and manage the expectations as to when you will reasonably be able to complete the tasks. This may look like sending an email to both managers, or if they are both in the office, pull them together and outline that you are more than able to carry out the tasks, and this is how long you anticipate it to take. Get their concurrence if this suits their timelines and let them decide between themselves on what is the order of priority for you. The managers who are tasking you may not be talking to each other, so you need to instigate the channel of communication and get clarity.

> ## YOUNG GUN PRINCIPLE
> Learn to say no or not yet when it comes to excessive tasks allocated to you. It will be more advantageous to set the expectation up front as to what you can do, rather than say you will and not deliver.

Preparedness is also key to maintaining organisation. Before you undertake a task, ensure that you have all that you need to execute it. And that means looking ahead at what you need to do. If there is an upcoming meeting, you will need to spend sufficient time in preparation for it, to maximise the effectiveness of it. Scrambling beforehand creates unnecessary stress. You will also be seen as more proficient when you prepare in advance. Lack of preparedness is what wastes time, when more effort needs to be exerted in the follow-up and rework. However, if your schedule is a mess and you are constantly in reactive mode to tasks that arise, you are limiting your ability to get ahead and look ahead. As noted by Benjamin Franklin, 'An ounce of prevention is worth a pound of cure.'

TRIGGER QUESTIONS

1. Do you have conscious awareness of where you invest your time? Where do you waste the most time?

2. Do you know when you work best? Is it during the morning, afternoon or evening?

3. Have you set up an organisational system between your work diary and Outlook? Is your time currently optimised?

4. Is there any duplication of effort that you can make redundant?

5. Do you spend most of your time responding to the demands of others or driving your own workload?

6. Do you make daily, weekly and monthly plans for your time or do you leave things to chance? What will be the benefit to your work by generating a plan?

7. When you get organised, do you stay organised? Why/why not?

YOUNG GUN BULLETS

- Block out time in your calendar to plan your day, week and month ahead. Creating a routine of doing this will become a long-standing habit that serves your time.
- Optimise your time by doing the meaningful and deep work when you work your best. Time-block your calendar using colours to indicate when you will be undertaking each type of work.
- Avoid hoarding files and papers, and work in a decluttered space. Take ten minutes once a week to reset your workspace instead of letting the paperwork pile up.

P

POLITICS

PŎL´Ĭ-TĬKS

INTRIGUE OR MANOEUVRING WITHIN A POLITICAL
UNIT OR A GROUP IN ORDER TO GAIN CONTROL OR
POWER

---

*'People sitting all day for hours looking at a glowing light
are bound to get ran over like a deer in headlights.' – Richie
Norton*

Corporate is politics. So don't be fooled that they're not one and
the same, you need to play the game if you intend to win. Only
a person with too much naivety would think that it's not, and
I was one of those people when I started off. Albeit politics was
touched on before, it's imperative to sharpen your mind to the
battlefield of corporate politics. The faster and further you want
to go, the more you will encounter this. This is an affliction of

126

all size companies, and you need to be as versed in politics as possible, because hard work and goodwill alone doesn't get you up the chain. That's what I thought, until I had a rude awakening that people in offices spend time vested in this, instead of focusing on enabling everyone to succeed and thrive. In a utopian world, this section would be rendered irrelevant. In its simplest form, workplace politics is about the differences between people at work – differences in opinions and conflicts of interest, and is reflected in workplace alliances, biases and relationships. By sheer virtue of being around a variety of people, there will be clashes and there will be those with misguided intentions. Shying away from it isn't the option, as you don't want to be caught off-guard, but ready and alert. Understanding the political landscape in an organisation is equivalent to understanding the culture within, both reflective of how things are done or not within the place. They are the subtle norms and expectations within a business.

YOUNG GUN PRINCIPLE
Don't get involved in workplace politics that have nothing to do with you. Consider yourself to always be Switzerland, and never take sides in a situation that has no relevance to you.

The intensity and complexity of politics that you experience will vary at the level you are at, but there are key political considerations that you can be aware of at the entry-level, nonetheless. Starting with:

1. Understanding the organisational chart. As a young gun there

may be hesitancy to talk to the seniors in the business, thinking that you have nothing to say or are lesser than because you are starting out. That's a limiting belief, but that shouldn't stop you from observing where the power and influence lies in an organisation. The personnel at the top, however, have their trusted advisors on the ground – that is, their eyes and ears who provide them with intel they need to make decisions, and unfortunately at times, they rely on this sole channel to form a perception about you (rightly or wrongly so). Understanding the organisational chart is also about seeing who gets a seat at the table, for these are also the decision-makers or have key influence in the business as well. And pay attention as to who is in the know. In a company I worked for, the office manager was the centre of all information, meaning, they had open lines of communication to the people of influence and power. Keeping your eyes and ears aware and in observation is imperative to you navigating the political landscape, because …

2. You can then build relationship equity. There is only one bank that is more valuable than the financial one, and that is the favour bank. The day you plant the seeds isn't the day you reap the crops, and it's the same with networking and building your relationship capital. Ensuring the right people in the business know you for how you want to convey yourself is essential. Actively seeking out opportunities for touch points and interactions with the aforementioned organisational personnel will aid you in the long run.

3. Don't make enemies. The construction industry is an extremely small industry, and your name will precede you. If you do bad by a handful of contractors, it will eventually come back

at you. If you purposely short pay, talk down, try and pull rank as a graduate over a contractor or subcontractor, you will soon start to have a list of people who won't work with you. The same goes within an organisation. Most people are quite short-sighted when they think they can get away with bad behaviour. It's not if they will get away with it, it's how long for. Don't engage in any subpar behaviours, it's that simple. This requires you to stick to your values and principles, even if the organisation or team you are in is compromised on them. You will always triumph in the long-term.

4. Learn to address the problem and not the person. Most politics start when people attack, discriminate or judge the person and not their behaviour or action. When you need to address a conflict or issue, ensure that you are isolating this from the person itself. When people feel personally attacked, that's when they will turn to political games. Ensure you are clear, concise and diplomatic when raising issues.

5. Seek to understand, before being understood. When you demonstrate that you have a thorough understanding and have also made a consolidated effort to understand the perspective of another person, you will gain an ally.

6. Think win-win. Most people are conditioned into thinking that if one person gains, the other loses, and this is what also fuels the perception that office politics is a bad thing. To win at politics is to follow the golden rule that everyone comes out on top. Playing the game isn't about looking at how you can defeat someone else, but how you can both win. This is the strategic approach instead of the bullish approach.

7. Work with facts and logical consistency rather than perception

and personal biases. When conversations about differences of any nature arise, there is a tendency for conversations to be based in the subjective. This is a dangerous territory as most people's feelings, perceptions and opinions change with the weather. If there is a conflict or difference, seek to first establish a mutually agreed common ground based on fact and not feeling.

8. Engaging in politics can fuel emotions. When emotions are triggered, what we can see is emotional tantrums and outbursts. This is a consequence of when people don't have strong mental fortitude and resilience to see the game for what it is – a game. It's imperative in any politically fuelled engagement to remain calm, poised and centred. If you need to vent, do so afterwards, and don't run out of the room bursting into tears (I speak from experience until I knew better). Maintain a stealth-like composure, and never let the emotions get the better of you in the heat of the moment.

9. And finally, play. If someone has engaged in a political battle with you, you need to play. You're not in the wrong, as you haven't initiated this, but you do need to defend your integrity and reputation. If the other side goes back to being neutral, so do you.

YOUNG GUN PRINCIPLE

The colloquialism of 'keeping your nose clean' is integral in playing politics. No-one can say a bad word about you if there's nothing to hold against you.

As a young gun, you can also assess how political an

organisation is by looking out for favouritism and nepotism. Favouritism is when managers or leaders provide special treatment and exemptions to employees for reasons wholly unrelated to their job performance. A survey conducted by Georgetown University's McDonough School of Business found that 92% of senior business executives have seen favouritism at play in employee promotions, including in their own companies (84%). About a quarter of the polled executives admitted to practicing favouritism themselves. Favouritism can become problematic, in that the results and competency of someone may be well overlooked in favour of a personal relationship. This can amount to missed promotions and opportunities. On the whole, this significantly hurts a company when people aren't being evaluated and valued on their results and contribution, not if they both play golf together on Sunday. Nepotism is the practice of appointing or promoting family members to positions which they are underqualified for, or there is someone else much more capable and deserving of that position. I worked on a project where a family member of a senior in that organisation went from a coordinator position to contract administrator position in less than a year having never independently tendered anything or processed a single claim. This caused significant friction amongst others, who have been aiming for promotion on merit and not surname for years, eventually causing them to leave. If you see that management can't distinguish favouritism from performance recognition, you can speak up. Always let your results speak for yourself and identify that even if this may be in existence, you're not barred from opportunity. However, you do need to consider your long-term objectives, and consider if favouritism or nepotism will present barriers to more scarce positions. This negative side of corporate politics has certainly caused people to move on, and ultimately, that may be the case for you if you've played all your cards right and still receive inequitable outcomes.

Corporate politics are just as any other brand of politics –they're about influencing, strategising, forming partnerships, enlisting allies, taking decisions, and at the end of the day, coming out on top. In business, that means achieving a milestone, a goal, getting something done or approved. The question that will provide a young gun the greatest point of differentiation is not just what you do, but how you do it. To win at the corporate game in the long-term is to have a deep and nuanced understanding of human psychology and develop advantageous relationship equity. Never get caught in crossfire that has nothing to do with you, and as aforementioned, never gossip. Whilst it can be tempting, a young gun should never engage in or pedal any gossip within a team environment. This weakens your position within a team. Funny thing, when a person resigns from a team, people immediately want to find out why and where they are going. I never asked or expressed curiosity on this, nor asked someone else onsite if they heard that X was leaving. It's none of my business. If you are talking ill of another colleague at lunch, it will form the impression that you will do the same of the people you are talking to. Talk of other people is also the lowest form of conversation, so abstain from it. If you do end up in such a conversation, leave if you can, or stay silent.

'Politics is the business of getting power and privilege without possessing merit.' – PJ O'Rourke

TRIGGER QUESTIONS

1. How well can you read a political landscape? Do you feel that you have a good understanding of what constitutes corporate politics?
2. How would you describe corporate politics in your current organisation?
3. Who are the people of influence in your organisation and industry? What do you think makes them influential?
4. How does your organisation handle sensitive and conflicting views? Are they open and accommodating or do they seek to maintain the status quo?
5. Are you sensitive to feedback and opinions of others? If yes, why?
6. Does the organisation have a track record of making equitable decisions or do you find they only favour a select group of people?

YOUNG GUN BULLETS

- Refine and sharpen your persuasion, negotiation and influencing skills as soon as you can. This can be done through mentoring and coaching programs or self-education such as books and podcasts.

- Identify the key people of influence in your organisation and come up with smart ways to build relationships with them. Proximity is key in attaining information and building visibility with the right people in the organisation.
- Observe how other people react around corporate politics, and if a situation arises, think of the core motives of the people involved. The more that you can unpack a situation and get to the core of an issue, the better you will be when it's your turn to play.

Q

QUESTIONS

KWĔS′CHƏN

A SENTENCE, PHRASE OR GESTURE THAT SEEKS

INFORMATION THROUGH A REPLY

'Judge a man by his questions rather than his answers.'
— Voltaire

A common concern that young guns have when they're starting is
the fear that they'll be found out for not knowing anything from
a technical perspective. Remember that they didn't hire you as
a cadet or graduate for your incredible technical aptitude. They
hired you for your cultural fit, ability to learn, hunger, curiosity
and how you think in given situations. No-one starts off knowing
all they need to know about their role. What's the fun in that? It's
even recognised in industry that once you enter and make a start,
you go through a period of unlearning everything they told you

in academia and start learning practice. Naturally, as your career progresses, there will be more weight on what you do know from a technical training perspective, but not at this stage. So, you can remove that pressure from yourself of needing pre-knowledge to fulfil your entry-level role. But what your new employers do expect you to do, is ask questions. Whilst this may seem obvious, there are some young guns who think this is a sign of weakness or it will become their unravelling and they'll be exposed for not knowing what to do. Assuredly, you'd be in a better position asking the question and proceeding with clarity, then proceeding on an assumption and having to explain in retrospect why you didn't ask the question.

'The wise man doesn't give the right answers, he poses the right questions.' – Claude Lévi-Strauss

A study done by the Harvard Business School found that asking questions in the workplace may cause others to view you as more engaged and intelligent. Although some may fear retribution or being seen as annoying, an inquisitive nature is often a sign of great competence. It's a career booster, not a career inhibitor. There are certain cultures or even particular upbringings that have ingrained in the minds of some that you should just do as you're told and stay silent. There's no place for that within a workplace, for if you don't ask, you simply won't learn – if you don't ask, you don't get. Our natural modality of learning is through asking questions, not quelling them. Asking questions also fosters the culture of collaboration and transparency of information, as cooperation is a natural outcome of asking questions. When you ask questions, it also forces you to think, as you are assessing the gaps in your knowledge. Understandable that at first, you may not know what the right questions are to be asking, so you can start with basic questions that will allow the conversation to progress. It can be as simple as, 'What do I need to know about X task before I carry on with it?' If you work on construction sites, you will find that there'll be ample heated scenarios, and the best way to diffuse this is through asking questions. People get frustrated when they feel that they aren't being heard, so asking questions will allow you to direct them away from their emotions and get the information that you need that will assist them to move forward.

YOUNG GUN PRINCIPLE

Express no hesitation in asking questions to enable you to have depth and breadth of understanding. Asking questions unlocks your learning.

Most people believe that there is no such thing as a stupid question. Of course, there is. It would be a stupid question to outright ask management for a pay rise. It would be a smart question to ask management for a meeting to discuss your long-term ambitions for the company and how we can work together to ensure we all meet our collective goals. It would be a stupid question to ask a contractor to drop an exorbitant amount off their quote. It would be a smart question to ask the contractor what their best and final offer is. The qualifier is also the context. If you can see that a person has had a rough day and hasn't been available all day, following them up on an outstanding task won't be the best approach. So, whilst there are stupid questions, the qualifier is the context. In your context, you're learning. So even if you do ask a question out of place or it didn't sound as you intended it to, you will only learn from the experience. Assuredly, people won't remember months on if you asked low-resolution questions a handful of times, so don't let that stop you from asking.

Business leaders are actively seeking those who can question everything. You need to get into the mindset early on of questioning everything. Take nothing for its face value. If you don't start questioning everything, you'll never prime your mind to find opportunities, see a niche for innovation. If you don't do this, you will be an employee for life, just waiting to be told what to do and what to think next. I agree that the professional marketplace is crowded; at the bottom, where the majority will sit around and wait for others to tell them what to do, and put in the bare minimum and expect the absolute maximum. Succeeding in your career isn't about your level of compliance to follow orders. A computer does that just fine. The issue with most people not having a willingness or open-mindedness to question everything is their lack of confidence to be wrong. So what, you're wrong. I assure you with where you are in your life right now, you're already wrong on so many things. You haven't gotten it right up until now, so why have this hesitation moving forward? If you are wrong, consider it a humbling opportunity to learn and grow. I am also willing to be proven wrong, because it means I have upgraded a belief and challenged an existing notion I had. If you can run into the discomfort of questioning everything and having the stamina to shatter everything you think you know in the ambition of improvement, you will be so far ahead of the masses, you'll even surprise yourself in the process.

Consider the following in any given scenario to be brilliant at asking questions:

- First, start with the end in mind. Research dating back to the 1970s found that conversations are had to accomplish some combination of two major goals: information exchange (learning) and impression management (liking). When you're going in for a conversation, be clear on what you're seeking to achieve. Is it facts and data? Or is it an opinion? This will allow you to start framing your questions.
- Avoid asking yes or no questions from the outset, you may end up with limited information. Questions that commence with 'should', 'would', 'are', 'do you think' and 'is' will lead to a yes/ no answer. Questions that are framed with 'who', 'what', 'when', 'where', 'why' and 'how' will start a detailed conversation.
- Through actively listening you'll be able to adequately follow up, which is how you progress a conversation through the stages of inquiry. To probe, or drill down, you can ask someone an 'exactly' question: 'What exactly is meant by …?' You can also ask rhetorical questions, far-fetched or imaginative questions, or leading questions, which are used to bring the respondent along your way of thinking.

There are two colloquialisms rampant in the construction industry. One, 'We've always done it that way,' and two, 'It is what it is.' Both statements automatically place a cap on thinking and questioning. I've heard few people ask why we have always done it that way. 'It is what it is' is terrible, as it allows people to accept low standards and not feel responsible or ignited to do anything about it. Plus, it suggests that best practice has been achieved, when we should always be aiming for better practice. When you hear these sayings float around your office or site, always ask why. As Chinese philosopher Confucius said, 'The man who asks a question is a fool for a minute, the man who does not ask is a fool for life.'

TRIGGER QUESTIONS

1. Do you consider asking questions a sign of weakness, thus holding yourself back?
2. Do you take the first response as a given, or do you probe and ask why?
3. Are you taking advantage of each conversation as a learning opportunity to ask questions?
4. How do you think your understanding and intelligence would benefit if you asked ten more questions a day than you normally would?
5. Are you afraid of the embarrassment of asking the wrong question? Is there such a thing as a wrong question, or does it need to be a more considered question?
6. What are the key mental limitations preventing you from asking more questions, and how can you change that narrative into a positive one?

YOUNG GUN BULLETS

- Quite simply, ask more questions. Set a mental rule that each time you aren't sure, you will ask the question.
- Actively take notes in your conversations, as it will enable you to pause and reflect on what is being said before you ask questions.
- Get into a habitual mindset of questioning everything and not taking things on face value or 'it is the way it is'. This is lazy thinking and doesn't fuel grounds for innovation and opportunity. Always think, *Why?*

R

RESULTS

RĬ-ZŬLT'

TO HAPPEN AS A CONSEQUENCE: SYNONYM:

FOLLOW

'Resources are hired to give results, not reasons.' – Amit Kalantri

Of the many wholescale changes I would apply to corporate, a key one would be assessing employees purely on their results, achievements and outputs. Where they would work, and how they would work, would be wholly open for discussion, as to facilitate the optimal environment to allow for outcomes to be generated. It would absolve many issues that go unresolved, such as pay equity. A person would be paid in direct relation to their contribution to the financial success of an organisation, the complexity of the problem they are solving or if they meet KPIs – bar administration and data entry type roles, to a certain extent. I can already hear the uproar – 'This isn't equitable.' It would require an individual to dramatically upskill themselves and not rely on sheer presenteeism to afford them a salary. Most employees would be finding, for the first time, they'll have to think independently and critically and more about the business needs than themselves. This would make a larger percentage of the workforce entrepreneurial minded, and rely on their creativity, resourcefulness and problem-solving to generate income. Don't reject the idea too soon, this is common in startups. As an entrepreneur, the only way we get paid is by demonstrating results. Income isn't coming in any other way. The remuneration that I bring into my business is a direct reflection of my mindset and skillset. I'm not promised any income unless I continually add value and solve problems. This isn't to encourage you to pursue entrepreneurship, but it is to encourage you to think that your salary isn't promised to you either, and the only way to ensure as best as possible its continuity, is to deliver results.

What is of equal importance in the pursuit of excellence is how you generate the result. As a young gun, you'll see subpar practices in the industry. I remember walking into the office of an executive at an organisation I worked for, who just got off the phone with a subcontractor telling him to complete the complimentary tiling works for the project manager in order to win a multimillion-dollar tender. Do you know what doesn't take any skill? Coercion and blackmail. Do you know what does take skill? Pricing a project that allows all parties to make a profit and successfully negotiating with a client on this. Going back to my earlier days in corporate, I would see project management personnel ensuring that the awarded trade package would also cover their latest set of renovations. The subcontractor was getting paid, for all they cared, so they kept meeting targets onsite. That's the subpar way of generating results on sites. On equal footing, there would be project managers who achieved results for the client, however with great collateral of diminished team spirit and culture, unsatisfied staff and shady dealings with contractors. Does this sound like industry best practice to you? No, it shouldn't. I could continue, as I've seen more than enough examples of people who promote integrity as a core value, yet their actions speak the opposite. As a young gun, do not get sucked into these types of dealings to achieve what you need to. Don't cut corners, you will not become more exemplary or excellent in doing so. You can do anything with the only two conditions of upholding moral and ethical boundaries. If a person can't achieve their desired outcome without doing this, they have a severe mindset and skillset deficiency. In the process of delivering results, don't create collateral damage. It's not just what you achieve, but how you achieve it that matters just as much. Of course, it's within your realm of possibility, as I have seen equal examples of personnel in the industry do just that.

> ## YOUNG GUN PRINCIPLE
> There is a direct correlation between the income you receive and the results you generate. Focus your attention on constantly achieving results to influence your income.

A principle that I use in my business to know what I need to focus on is the Pareto principle. The Pareto principle determines that 80% of consequences and outcomes come from 20% of causes. This is also known as the 80/20 rule. This principle was founded through Pareto's observation of wealth and population, where 80% of the land in Italy (then) was owned by 20% of the population. The idea for a young gun is to focus on the 20% of their tasks or functions that will result in 80% of the impact, value and results. Without a method of assessing what is important out of everything that is unimportant, you won't deliver as much as you can. I know within my work that these key functions must be delivered on to get the greatest results. Everything else is secondary or needs to be outsourced. You can use this same method of assessment when looking at your to-do list to identify where to concentrate your time and efforts to get the greatest results.

It will always be advantageous to work to your strengths. Working to your strengths means engaging in work that you are exceptionally good at and comes naturally to you. This is referred to as operating in your zone of genius. Your zone of genius is when you lose track of time, remain energised and aren't aware of your bodily requirements when you're carrying out a work function. When I am mentoring or coaching, speaking, delivering workshops, writing books, I completely lose track of time. My energy flows, and when I engaged in these activities, I would, and do, feel energised and intrinsically driven to produce value and results. Even within each of these activities, I know where my strengths are. When podcasting, my strength is in speaking and interviewing, not in audio production. When I play to my strengths in the tasks that I am engaged with and outsource the rest, I have more mental space available to add more value, generate more results, and the cycle continues. On the other hand, it is a mental nightmare for me to engage in technical and detailed work. A stretch claim coming from someone who worked in construction. I always preferred dealing with people and numbers than technical details. However, when I had to engage in it, sometimes half an hour would feel like three hours. The results that I would generate weren't maximised. In your workplace, put your hand up for tasks and roles that allow you to play to your strengths for as much of a percentage as possible. You will be more successful at your job if 50% of your role is strengths-based, instead of 20%. Without doing a deep dive into your personality and natural disposition, pay attention to patterns in your performance, what you enjoy doing the most at work, and reflect on how your energy rises or falls to find out where your strengths are.

'You don't get any medal for trying something, you get medals for results.' – Bill Parcells

Parallel to knowing your strengths is knowing what motivates you. It's a blind spot in corporate environments that assumes everyone is motivated by the same thing. In eight years in corporate, not once was I asked what motivates me. To enable your management team to get the best results out of you, you will have to tell them what that is. To some, gratitude and words of appreciation motivate them to strive for more. For others, they want time off, and others, simply fill up their bank accounts. Heard of the love languages? Well, they apply to the workplace as well. A young gun needs to know what makes them feel good at work for doing good work. Leverage and articulate this to keep on doing great work. Know what adds fuel to your fire that will always allow you to go that rhetorical extra mile. You will also be naturally motivated and inspired to do work that is meaningful. If you can't reason with yourself as to why you are doing what you are, then it's time to go back to constructing your career.

Whilst this whole book is written in the context of generating results, don't forget the following in the pursuit of results:

- Have focus to finish what you start. A scattered mind creates scattered time, and you just end up handling the same task repeatedly.
- Do not confuse productivity with results. You may be working twelve-hour days but have the same to show as someone working eight-hour days. It's not just the efficiency factor but how effective you are and how intensive your efforts are in generating results. Refer to O for Organisation for a recap on what to focus on.
- A key piece of advice I tell my constructors who are approaching interviews is to focus on the process and the results will come. You have the most control over the process, and when your attention is tuned to that, your results will come.
- As a rule of thumb, where you spend the most time and energy along with developing your skillset will you get results. Best practice is to reverse-engineer the process by first determining which results you seek, to determine the time and energy contribution required to achieve it through mindset and skillset mastery.

As a pinnacle to attaining results is solving problems. As

mentioned before, the level of remuneration, progression and recognition you experience is reflective of the complexity of the problem you solve. If you want to influence your income, you first need to seek how you can add more value to others. The first pitfall those with linear, institutionalised thinking have when approaching problems is not addressing the root cause of the problem but treating the symptom. Half the challenge of solving a problem is to clearly pinpoint and define it. To then solve it, the problem needs to be assessed from multiple angles, zooming in and out to truly capture all the factors at play. When people are brainstorming solutions, the key is to be open-minded and not discount any solution. A team of engineers were tasked with absorbing a massive oil spill that happened in a gulf area. The sheer volume was unlike they've ever dealt with beforehand, and time was against them as the spill was impacting the environment. One engineer jokingly said to throw in penguins, as the oil sticks to their feathers. After they laughed at the notion, they realised that's what they needed – absorbers that performed like penguins (certainly not real penguins). Dismissing a prospective solution too prematurely because of your own limitations and biases can elongate the problem-solving process. Once the solution is implemented, it must be monitored and controlled, for only real-time data and results are the measure of the effectiveness of the solution. Ensure that clear KPIs are established during the solution process so all parties can coherently assess the outcome.

Lastly, when solving problems, you need to get as much exposure in the first instance as to *how* others around you solve problems. Most people have a shallow approach to solving problems. They do a quick identification of the problem and immediately want to come to a solution. You need to get as much exposure to the critical thinking and line of questioning and assessment that comes up when seniors around you are solving problems. Don't just wait around for a solution, but learn the *how*. Problem-solving with real-time application is a highly refined skill, and the more variety of scenarios that you can get exposure to, the better for your critical thinking and application in the long run.

Results don't lie and do more talking to your name than you ever can. And results generate and beget more results. You get momentum, and with consistent application of effort and discipline, eventually you'll have more results to your name so that catching up or competing with you takes a monumental effort. No-one can take your results away from you and will always enhance your ability to standout and succeed.

TRIGGER QUESTIONS

1. Are you satisfied with the results you've achieved for yourself to date? Why/why not?
2. Do you know why you are doing what you are doing most of the time?
3. Do you limit the level of action you take because of potential obstacles along the way? Are you easily defeated by setbacks and roadblocks?
4. Are you clear on the metrics of assessing your results? Do you have a clear way of measuring your results?

5. Who do you need to become to have the massive results that you seek to achieve?
6. How are you ensuring that you stay focused on the outcomes despite the journey to the destination being rough and long-winded?

YOUNG GUN BULLETS

- Before proceeding with any task, visualise the outcome that you want to achieve daily. Feel how it would feel if you'd achieved the result you are seeking before it happens. Do this as often and as intensely as you can until you experience it in real life.
- When experiencing a setback or a roadblock, limit the amount of time you are knocked back. If it hasn't gone according to plan, change the method but not the goal. The faster you can get back on the proverbial horse and keep going, the more results you will attain for yourself.
- When setting the outcome you want to achieve, stretch the outcome. If you aim higher than where you originally intended, you will still be better off if you fall short from your stretch goal than your original goal. For example, if you say you want to go to five networking events, make the target ten. If you end up at seven events, you are still better off than the initial five you started with.

S

SITE LIFE

SĪT

THE PLACE WHERE A STRUCTURE OR GROUP OF
STRUCTURES WAS, IS, OR IS TO BE LOCATED

'You can use an eraser on the drafting table or a
sledgehammer on the construction site.' – Frank Lloyd Wright

On one of the commercial projects I worked on, a new cadet had
just joined the site. I remember my excitement and anticipation
when I was first being moved to site full-time. Not that I had
a clue as to what I would really be doing, but it felt grand and
instilled a sense of importance. I observed that over the few days
since the cadet started, no-one was providing him with guidance,
nor did he really know what to do. It's a graduate's dream to work
onsite, and then come the opportunity, they're automatically
glued to the screen as they were in head office. This is a bad habit

established at the outset of many young guns' careers, as they work onsite, but are never actually onsite. To enable long-term success in the industry, one must learn building construction in the most practical sense of the term. And this requires a conscious and concentrated effort to go out to the physical building site and observe, monitor, query and absorb the construction works happening. When starting out onsite, it can get very easy to be swept up in the apparent urgency of the low-level (important, but low-level) tasks a cadet gets handed. And it's usually the tasks that others onsite haven't had the time for. The onus is on you to prioritise your learning and development above what others deem as priorities for you (refer back to P for Preparation for guidance on time management and allocation).

I, myself, have been guilty of this many times during my tenure on sites, especially in the winter months. However, you don't learn building construction through a site office. You learn construction through physically being on the construction site, not 100% in the site shed. The lesson here is simple – get out onsite. On the first project I was running and based out onsite, I made a one-off decision that I would do a site walk each morning before turning on my laptop. It was a non-negotiable, and I didn't remake the decision every single day, it was a given. By going out to site before you open your laptop, you won't get sucked into the vortex of emails and tasks set by others as a graduate. In a whole working day, I assure you, you have the time to print all the updated drawings that have come in *and* spend thirty minutes onsite. The benefit of doing one daily site walk as a minimum, was that I could see the progress from the previous day and start to get a true sense of appreciation as to durations, access considerations and all the nuances that don't appear on paper when something needs to be installed six metres in the air. I would stand and watch slabs being prepped and poured. A structural slab drawing isn't going to tell you that a pour has a minimum crew of eight and what each one of them is responsible for. And you need to know the number of men required for a pour, because one day you may get a variation for additional works and need to assess it based on your own knowledge and experience. As bland as it may sound to you from the outset, I encourage you to first stand and watch concrete pours, precast erection, a stud wall being erected (and so on). But even more so, ask questions and engage with the trades or management responsible for carrying out the works. This is how you learn building construction, not just from all the supporting activities and tasks like reading plans, specifications, meetings, RFIs and the like.

YOUNG GUN PRINCIPLE

Make a scheduled and conscious effort to go out to site every morning and at the end of the day. Block out this time in your calendar and set a reminder and attend to it like you would if this were a scheduled meeting with other participants.

Of course, as a newbie to site, it can feel daunting to just head out to site by yourself. So take the initiative and ask the site manager, project manager or any other project personnel to take you out to site or if you can shadow and join them when they next go. It's best practice to spend as much time as possible observing site managers in action. They're the ones responsible for the immediate/short-term onsite coordination and planning of the works and are the trades' first point of call for any issues. You will learn more from tailing an excellent site manager about construction in a few weeks than the whole of your degree. By shadowing them, you will observe how they work through problems and coordination issues on the spot. What are they considering? What are the potential flow-on effects to other trades if, say, a duct gets lowered? It's not just technical problems that they deal with, but also a lot of personality issues. It was very confronting for me to see a yelling match happen onsite the first time round, only to unfortunately realise that's how some choose to communicate – in volume rather than words. Some site and project managers will have the foresight to take you by the hand out onsite, but not all will. So put your hand up and ask for the learning opportunity. I assure you it won't be met with objections.

The best sites are those that are safe. Never be mistaken – every single person on a construction site has the right to attend work and leave safely, and as they came. No priority, demand or task ever comes above the health and safety of a worker onsite, no matter which company they work for. Every person onsite has a responsibility to ensure this is the case. It's a common saying within the industry that the standard you walk by is the standard you accept. If you know that a person should be wearing a hard hat, tell them. It's common as a cadet onsite to feel that you don't have the authority to tell someone to do that, but when it comes to safety, everyone does. As I write this, I recall a project where I was mainly responsible for the fit-out works. There was a plasterer who made it his duty to be lax with his hard hat wearing. It just so happened that each time he happened to be lax in doing so, I would walk by. I used multiple approaches, but he wouldn't consistently comply. It got to the point where I told him he'd sit a reinduction the next morning. I certainly felt uncomfortable using that card on him, but it worked, and he wore the hat.

The benefit of commencing your career with larger tier one or two companies is their dedication, systems and processes to manage health and safety onsite. I've worked with foremen who've come up through companies commonly referred to as cowboys of the industry where handrails weren't seen on any roofs, and no single safe work method statement was ever sighted. If you end up on a site where there are little to no health and safety considerations, I encourage you to take it into your own hands to learn so via enquiring within and possibly seeking further external training. If you are on a site with dedicated health and safety professionals, then attend the weekly safety walks, as you will learn how to read a site through their safety framework and become nuanced and well-trained in identifying risks and hazards. I have also noticed that sites that implement safety systems through rewarding great behaviour instead of punishing bad behaviour have performed well and have had less repeat offenders.

A major part of implementing safety onsite is understanding human psychology and herd mentality. This takes time to observe and internalise, so ensure that you are proactive in your approach to health and safety. Depending on the company size, as a cadet, you will primarily be tasked with running the inductions and safety administration anyways, but the mountain of paperwork that daily awaits you is not an excuse for not physically going out to site.

'It is not the beauty of a building you should look at; it's the construction of the foundation that will stand the test of time.'
— David Allan Coe

A skill that is being lost with this generation of constructors is the ability to draw details. The majority of the people you are dealing with on sites, especially trade, communicate information, details and methodologies through drawing details. What do you think is more powerful on a construction site – drawing a footing cross-section detailing the reo spacing and marking up concrete strength or writing a whole paragraph on this? The former, naturally. I have found that learning to communicate details via drawing was best learnt off trades. If they had a question, I'd ask them to draw it for me, and I would go and reiterate the sketch in my own terms to ensure I understood the detail before I would pass it on in an RFI (request for information). Considering that you are dealing with a myriad of stakeholders that don't just speak different languages, but all have different communication styles, there is one language on construction sites that is universal – drawings. When you are requesting clarification or wanting to pass on instruction as to how a certain trade, contractor or consultant should proceed, a detailed drawing or mark-up makes it clear and concise. The written word can be open to interpretation. It's happened before, when a contractor proceeded on the written interpretation of an instruction to the best of their understanding, which was installed correctly, however, it was also the more expensive approach. There were little grounds to argue the price after the fact, as they'd received the written instruction with no accompanying sketch. Even if you don't attach a drawing, do make sure that the instruction can only be interpreted in one way. To have this level of technical acumen requires you to – you guessed it – get out onsite. If you haven't seen how three steel beams are connected to one column, it may be difficult to detail the plate connection and weld type if you don't have a built-up visual dictionary that you can reference. And if you don't understand something being explained to you onsite, have them draw it for you.

As you have progressed through the alphabet of this guide, and as your days onsite increase, you'll start connecting the dots and seeing more opportunities to maximise your learning, development and time onsite. The key for you is to be proactive in getting exposure to as much building construction activity as possible and not be holed up behind a desk or in a shed. If you are starting out within a consultancy, and not a head contractor, naturally the exposure to site is reduced. You can still take the principles within this section and apply it to your relevant work situation. For example, if you have started off as an assistant project manager working client side, ensure that you go out to site whenever the opportunity avails, and when you are there, ask the builder as many questions as possible. You could even coordinate your time and strike a deal – on the proviso you get your work done on time and meet your deliverables, you could spend an extra few hours out onsite. There really aren't set rules around this, you're only limited by your own thinking and ingenuity to make this work for you.

TRIGGER QUESTIONS

1. Do you truly enjoy working on a construction site, or do you prefer the office environment or a combination of both?

2. Are you working on a construction site but never leave the shed compound? How can you proactively participate in site activities?

3. Are you aware of all the preliminary site establishment requirements, from dealing with authorities to setting up all plans, right through to project completion? It is extremely beneficial to be involved in a project from tender handover to practical completion. Who do you need to flag this to within your organisation to get the right experience in a full project lifecycle?

4. Are you aware of the nuances of the chosen construction methodology and procurement framework? I.e. a construction management contract has different obligations than a design, novate or construct. Ensure you know the practical application and not just the theoretical.

5. Do you know the key risks and hazards involved in the project through its different cycles?

6. Are you familiar with the project contract, scope of works and responsibilities of the organisation in this project?

YOUNG GUN BULLETS

- If you are site-based, schedule a recurring event every morning and every afternoon for twenty minutes to go onsite and shadow a contractor, manager or any personnel working onsite. Ask them questions and get their detailed take on what they're working on. If there is terminology you aren't clear of, either ask or make a note to ask someone later. You can also ask to shadow relevant management when they go out to site, just ask the question.

- Take the initiative to generate your own minor works program. Even if it is for an activity that has already occurred, take your observations and put them into a program. It will enable you to build your acumen in sequencing and understand the relationship between different trades and durations. If you intend to work up to project management, programming is a key skill that is sought after.

- Join toolbox meetings and weekly site safety walks. It's imperative you also learn to view a construction site through an industrial relations and health and safety lens. Safety is everyone's duty. If you aren't site-based, ensure you maximise your time onsite and ask questions pertinent to site safety.

T

TEAMWORK

TĒM′WÛRK″

COOPERATIVE EFFORT BY THE MEMBERS OF A
GROUP OR TEAM TO ACHIEVE A COMMON GOAL

---

*'Talent wins games, but teamwork and intelligence wins
championships.' – Michael Jordan*

What is something that is imperative in the workplace, yet
no-one truly teaches you how to do it? Teamwork. There's excessive talk about high-performance teams, or even the importance
of teamwork, but little education up-front on the practicalities
of being a 'teamplayer'. Whilst it may sound like an obvious
behaviour, remember that there were people in your assignment
group at university who didn't pull their weight. An important
consideration of teamwork is that the company you work for first
has a responsibility to provide you with the right environment to

succeed. I wrote about this in my book, *Leadership in Construction.*
Leaders have the onus to set up their people for success, and this
also includes the provision of fair and equitable opportunities
which include people and projects for their teams to thrive. As
a young gun, you should have consistent conscious awareness of
placing yourself in environments and teams where you have the
greatest chance to succeed. I know that I do better in small teams,
as I prefer to be a big part of a small project. When put into the
opposite environment, I know that the success rate drops. The
career lesson at large is to know your person and what will enable
you to thrive.

YOUNG GUN PRINCIPLE
Being part of a team is never about compromising your
ideals, ideas or individuality, but finding the strength and
support within a team to express that.

Being a team player is an overused buzzword, with the conventional perspective that to be a team player, an individual cares
more about the team goals than their own success. This is a
conventional perspective. More powerful teams are those that
take into consideration what everyone seeks to achieve and ties
that into the overall ambition and goals of the team. Overall, an
individual shouldn't compromise any aspect of themselves to 'fit
in' to a team. The power of the collective is in the diversity of
perspectives, ideas and thoughts. That is the real balance; holding
your individuality and being part of a team. Being a team player
isn't about diminishing yourself to fit in. It is, however, about:

- Understanding what your role is and how you contribute to the overall running of the team. Think of a team as a machine, with everyone playing an imperative mechanism to its overall operation. Ensure that you are always clear what your place is within the team.
- Taking on extreme ownership and responsibility for your part. If you were assigned a task, don't wait around for someone else to finish it for you.
- Letting others assist. As a young gun, you may certainly want to display your independence and capability, but let others assist you where you need. This works twofold, in that a team is there to enable each other to achieve whatever their pursuit is.
- Allowing people within the teams to play to their strengths. It's easier to get a high-performance team when the right people are working on aligned tasks and opportunities. There's little merit telling a square peg to fit in a round hole, and if they can't achieve it then they need to change and improve or work harder. If a person on a team is better at contracts and numbers, don't have them dedicated to coordination and quality assurance.
- Instilling heightened transparency. A major contributor to why trust is low within teams is attributable to the lack of transparency. It's not a team-building day where you complete a murder mystery that builds trust, but ongoing transparency. Unnecessary meetings behind closed doors, not providing information in a timely manner or not being open about the trajectory of a project reduces trust. If a mistake is made, be transparent about the event all the same.

- Having a flexible approach to project demands, as well as flexing to others' work styles. As a young gun, you will be doing more flexing at first to get on the right side of management. Some project managers will bail you up on the phone as they're driving, others may make a five-minute conversation a forty minute one, others will get straight to the point. Work in with other management styles only on the proviso it's best practice and doesn't break any moral or ethical grounds.

- Being a team member with no agenda. This is pertaining to the world of corporate politics. Politics and its relationship to the workplace has been discussed, however, high-performance teams never seek to blame one another or get someone to do something in the name of an ulterior motive, agenda or to trip them up.

- Taking a collaborative, not just cooperative, approach. What's the difference? Collaborating is working together to achieve a common goal and coming together, whereas cooperation is defined as the actions of someone who is being helpful by doing what is asked of them. Someone who is truly collaborative will rarely say 'that's not my job' and focus on what they need to do to achieve the common goal.

- Making an effort to participate and engage with the team. To do this, it does assist if you like the people you work with. If you don't like them, respecting their position is a minimum. But if there's no like and respect, it'll be additionally difficult to participate and engage with your team. This also means taking a legitimate interest in the person. Few take the time to get to know the whole person, including the person outside of work. It's this connection that creates a team bond, not ad hoc team building days. Yes, you may be shy being new, but you will be spending the majority of your waking hours with these people, so get to know them.

These approaches are applicable upstream and downstream, and when implemented within the workplace, will allow you to quickly demonstrate teamwork which is a factor that is imperative to project delivery success. Being a team member is different to being a blind follower. The latter certainly doesn't contribute to the effectiveness of the team. If you find yourself in a team with unclear goals and directions, ask for clarifications. What's important within teams is not just to develop enthusiasm and focus but to maintain it. Especially over longer projects, people can start to lose inspiration or not see the finish line. Encourage change and innovation, and extend additional support if you can identify that the team morale is waning. Teams are not static entities, they're live ones that constantly require reinvigoration. Now, who said teamwork makes the dream work again …

'The strength of the team is each individual member. The strength of each member is the team.' – Phil Jackson

TRIGGER QUESTIONS

1. Do you like managing people and processes, or do you have a natural tendency to think bigger picture and more high level?
2. Do you generally prefer to work as part of a team or more

independently? What does this say about the type of role you should be in?

3. When teams are formed, what role do you organically play? Do you naturally gravitate towards the leadership role or do you prefer to take a backseat, implementation role? What does this say about your strengths?

4. How do you deal with underperforming or unmotivated team members? Do you do their work and share the credit or do you assist them?

5. How would other people describe your attitude and participation in teams? Would you agree with their assessment? Extra points for those who actually go and ask their colleagues to describe this.

6. Are you clear on the metrics that make teams successful? Reflect on teams that you have been in in the past; what has worked well? What hasn't worked well?

YOUNG GUN BULLETS

- Lead by example even if you are not the leader. Take the opportunity to display best practice team behaviour. This will demonstrate to the team that you can go above and beyond what's expected, plus holding yourself to higher standards without anyone telling you to.
- Consciously build trust with your team members, and on the grassroot level, this means doing what you say and saying what you will do. Without trust you'll be working twice as hard for half the reward.

- Write out the collective team rules and values that have been collaboratively generated and place it where team members can see it. You can include this at the start of meeting minutes to remind everyone of the commitment and expected performance.

U

UNIQUE

YŬ-ˈNĒK

A UNIQUE THING; A THING UNPARALLELED

OR SOLE OF ITS KIND

'To be yourself in a world that is constantly trying to make you something else is the greatest accomplishment.'
– Ralph Waldo Emerson

There is a deep significance to being unique in a world that funnels everyone to conformity and makes it extremely difficult to be all of who you are. Your individuality is a priceless possession and a gift from the creator. Whilst being genuine and being all of who you are have been touched on in B and X, I considered again and again if U should be for Unique. But that's exactly what a young gun is – unique. There wouldn't be a need to write a book about young guns if that was the status quo. In all my conversations with business leaders, the pain point of not being able to find incredible people is consistent. Because in a world that mass produces and commoditises, being unique is attractive in many ways and forms. Why does the marketplace more value on a Cartier watch than a Swatch watch? They both tell time. Except one is rare and exquisitely crafted and the other is available to anyone. One is more unique than the other, and society places more value on what is rare and unique than immediately available.

YOUNG GUN PRINCIPLE

Embrace your uniqueness and make it an ongoing discovery journey to identify all that makes you, you. Conformity is not within the lexicon of a young gun, for young guns will see where the majority are heading and see how they can head the other way.

A pivotal key to standing out and being successful is to live in alignment with your purpose. Think about it – out of all the people in the world, not a single other individual has the construction of you. No-one has the same combination that makes you. No two people can ever have the same experiences, beliefs, physical composition, behaviour, personality and the like. There are certainly similarities between you and others, but the sum of your whole is only found in you. It can't be that every person in construction has the parallel passion of delivering projects to time cost and quality and appeasing client expectations. Is this what you were put on this earth to do or is this what your organisation wants you to say? Naturally when most people come up through conventional academic systems (myself included) there is no exploration of self which allows for the discovery of your core purpose. No-one can dictate your purpose for you. The process of finding it out is one of self-discovery and that needs to happen alone. You can get mentors and coaches to guide you in the direction of finding it, but only you can look inwards to identify what that is. Each human being that is put on this earth has a unique mission, and it's their duty to find it. It's hidden deep within you, the place where most people look the least. We are that unique, that each one of us has been bestowed a unique mission and vision that only we can complete based on all of who we are. And it takes courage to explore your purpose and then even more courage to then make it your life's work.

Whilst I enjoyed working on project delivery, it wasn't my purpose. My dominant traits and natural disposition aren't to be technically orientated, and I take no joy from managing people, only leading people. I don't enjoy rigidity, and corporate structures are just that. I didn't feel purposeful enough simply being on project delivery. But when I stepped into my purpose of Thought Leadership, the world started to align. I stepped into my prerogative of being front-facing and the career success and growth that I've experienced in the last two years trumps the eight years of corporate combined. It's your duty to turn on your exploratory mind and uncover what it is that you are uniquely bestowed to be and do during this lifetime, for that is the key that will unlock the most stand-out success. You aren't here to be entertaining anything less than your purpose.

If you look at those who have achieved immense credibility and success in their chosen career path, they haven't played by the rules. There is no need to follow what the majority are doing. You may find that as you develop and continue to express your individuality, you won't be able to fit into prescribed boxes and standard-issue templates for having a career in construction. It's never for you to shrink your dreams to suit your current reality but to expand your current reality to match your dreams. There are multiple ways to have a career in construction, from venturing into the entrepreneurship realm, the Thought Leadership realm or a hybrid. I do love it when people can't stick labels on me to simplify what I do. I do many things in my career, and I love the diversity of it all. However, what I do today wasn't available as a role or a ready-made path walked by others in this industry. I had to pioneer it, for myself, and others. It takes immense strength and courage to not conform and to swim against the stream. I share this with you to build a sense of anticipation that a one-size-fits-all career doesn't work, and you will need to construct your career to suit your natural talents, passion, purpose, strengths and vision. If this can be found in employment, then great, however, that's not the only path for those who cannot and will not conform. What's imperative as you progress through your journey is to be in-tune with where you are. Do you feel that you've outgrown your current role? Do you have a nagging longing for something else? Listening to yourself is key to appreciating your uniqueness. Never let anyone tell you it's weird, unheard of, or as aforementioned, that you should be more like everyone else. Protect your uniqueness and build your career and life around it. As there is no-one else like you, you're just about guaranteed to stand out and achieve success on your own terms should you live in alignment with yourself.

A quality that is remarkably unique within the younger

generation is the ability to play the long-term game. Society has conditioned people to expect things immediately. Need food – Uber. Need a show – Netflix. Need money – Venmo. Need a date – Bumble. Everything is just about within arm's reach, just set up a profile, link your credit card, and it all arrives at your door. This conditions people to get used to an immediate cause and effect relationship. However, in the professional world, it doesn't happen like this. Instead of individuals committing to a long-term play, they seek quick wins and thrills. For example, leaving an organisation where there could have been partnership opportunities to work on the shiny new project. Executives are always on the lookout for who will take over. They got to where they are *because* they played the long-term game. Who is going to be the next generation to take over the business – they won't and can't be around forever. Most people go in and out of work on autopilot, with blinders to the opportunities and value they can add to business owners, if they just played the strategic long-term game. Plus, right now we're in the midst of 'The Great Resignation', with more and more people on the rise seeking to start a small business. Executives and business leaders are extremely keen to have talent on their team that they can nurture and groom to be the next business leader. Start thinking in ten-year timeframes, not ten minutes and certainly think beyond your plan for next weekend or Friday night. This alone will start putting great degrees of separation between you and your co-workers, and catch the attention of your organisational leaders. You can demonstrate your long-term play not just with your actions, and certainly not tenure alone, but openly expressing your plans and intentions and bringing innovation, value and opportunity to the table, that you, of course, want to be part of.

'The individual has always had to struggle to keep from being overwhelmed by the tribe. If you try it, you will be lonely often and sometimes frightened. But no price is too high to pay for the privilege of owning yourself.'–Friedrich Nietzsche

Like waves hitting the cliff shore, your personality and uniqueness will erode in corporate structures unless you make the conscious decision to not conform. Have the strength and courage to stand alone when you need to.

TRIGGER QUESTIONS

1. Do you feel that you've never fit in throughout your life?
2. How often do you think about your purpose? Why is it important to you to discover your purpose?
3. Why do you think it's important for you to discover what truly makes you unique?
4. What resources do you require to go on the self-discovery journey? Do you think a mentor or coach can provide you with the path of least resistance?
5. What will happen if you lose yourself and your uniqueness as your career progresses?
6. Do you seek quick thrills and immediate gratification? Or can you defer gratification in the long-term pursuit of your goals and ambition?

YOUNG GUN BULLETS

- Increase the number of people in your life and/or interactions with people who are leading their career and life on their own terms. Look for those who stand out in a sea of sameness and bring them into your immediate circle.

- Take a piece of paper and write out fifty things about yourself which are reflective of your personality, attitudes, actions, passions, tastes, perspectives and habits. Extra points if you can write out one hundred. For example, *I am the person who automatically takes lead in groups,* or, *I appreciate the finer things in life and choose quality over quantity.*

- Upon reflecting on the above, deeply consider what your unique purpose is in this lifetime. Can you narrow it down to certain functions?

V

VISIBILITY

VĬZ″ə-BĬL′Ĭ-TĒ

THE FACT, STATE OR DEGREE OF BEING VISIBLE

---

*'Those who work hard and constantly seek to be visible to
their superiors, those who showcase their hard work, are
the ones who advance to positions of greater power and
responsibility.'*
– Abhishek Ratna

As I was considering what V should be, I received a call from
a past constructor who completed my program. They're working in industry and called to get my advice on a few scenarios
that arose at work. One was that they'd completed a set of
tasks given, but the credit from the manager went to someone else. Putting aside that this is poor management, this
surprised my client. They'd done the work, why was someone

else being acknowledged? That was their first lesson to the importance of self-promotion. What isn't in your control is the quality and calibre of leaders and managers around you. Of course, they *should* recognise those that are excelling, but that doesn't mean that they will. What is in your locus of control is how you stand up for your own efforts and self-promote your achievements. No-one is going to come and do this for you, not offline and not online. Of course, this is done in a credible and notable fashion, and not in a bullish way that would come across as self-absorbed. But if you aren't highlighting all the amazing work you're doing, how will anyone know about it? Most have negative connotations with self-promotion, but this is a limiting belief and internalisation of beliefs that were constructed by the average in society and serve no benefit to you. Most people who adhere to this perceive that they can rely purely on diligence and merit to afford them the recognition, progression and remuneration in their career. If you do your best work in the dark, who is going to see it?

The mere act of standing out requires self-promotion. Remember, no-one wakes up in the morning thinking about you, only you do. That's why having a personal brand is essential, as it allows the essence of you to be clearly understood, and by mere fact of showing up congruently and authentically you will already be more distinct amongst those who have no idea who they are. Being another face in the crowd is not a strategy for success. Whilst young guns may not have immediate confidence to promote themselves, and usually take the approach of flying under the radar, you will be sorely disappointed to progressively go unnoticed, and the credit will go to those who are doing less than you.

YOUNG GUN PRINCIPLE

Adopt the mindset of a salesperson, for you are constantly selling the most valuable service of them all: you. This function is not beneath you, but imperative to you standing out for success.

The old adage of good work speaks for itself has become irrelevant and archaic. Self-promotion isn't an act of self-service. It would be a disservice to your team and organisation if they didn't know what an asset you are. When they realise how brilliant you are and the valuable contribution you make, it will benefit everyone involved. It's a disadvantage to management if they don't realise what a young gun they have in their midst. When you shift the perspective of self-promotion from 'it's about me' to 'it's about serving others', you'll start to be more inclined to consistently engage in it. Here are seven ways that you can self-promote your efforts and achievements at work in a subtle and credible manner:

1. Relay your achievements in real time with specificity. Instead of telling your manager, 'I have completed the measure,' say, 'I have completed the measure and found multiple discrepancies. I've accounted for those in the take-off, and were it not found, would have resulted in tens of thousands of dollars of exposure in the quote.' If you were to say the first sentence, your manager will

simply thinking, *Good.* However, in the second version, your manager is more likely to see the quality of your efforts and the positive repercussions it has on their efforts to meet commercial outcomes. Avoid being vague and nondescript when relaying your accomplishments, and always focus on the result and the outcome and the benefit of this to the business.

2. Maximise small talk and chance interactions. Instead of wasting the necessary small talk in the office on the bane and unimportant, use it to talk about what you are working on, how it is going and if there are any wins along the way. You will start to promote that you are invested in the success of the business and take your work seriously, whilst showing that you do truly care. This conversation trumps which football team won on the weekend. A short but powerful encounter with the right people in the organisation can open pathways.

3. Avoid deflecting praise. You can still be humble whilst accepting praise, there is no need to deflect it. Plus, when you deflect it, you are energetically sending out the vibe that this isn't what you want, and that you aren't worthy of a compliment, which will over time reduce your confidence as you continue to shrink yourself. If you receive a compliment, privately or publicly, say thank you and move on. There is no need for excessive modesty. This goes hand in hand when you share your accomplishments. There's no need to engage in self-depreciation – like you working sixteen-hour days for the last two weeks to get a tender over the line is not a worthwhile feat. Research by the American Psychological

Association found that humblebragging reduces how your competency is perceived and can contribute to others disliking you. Own your achievements and success proudly, for they haven't come in vain.

4. Be generous in giving praise to others. If it was a team effort, give credit to whoever worked with you to achieve the outcome. When others see you as generously giving praise, the law of reciprocity will come into play, and if they are equally good people, they'll work to make a point of acknowledging you and your successes without you having to say a word anymore. However, this comes from extending generosity first and adding value to others. This can also extend to aiding your colleagues if your schedule and workload allows for it.

5. When you are in a corporate presentation or meeting, and the presenter asks if anyone has any questions, there is usually dead silence. The effectiveness of being the first person to applaud and ask questions has been researched to showcase your affiliation for the organisation which is important in hierarchical cultures, which organisations are. And assuredly, the presenter will appreciate the reprieve of having to fish around for questions. Put your hand up and ask a meaningful question, and when the presentation is over, tell your colleague/presenter what you found insightful and engage in a brief conversation with a few additional questions. This will create a memorable impression because few to none do this.

6. As we live in the hyper-connected social age, promoting yourself outside of work has benefits in work. It may not come up in conversation that you went to an industry event

or are involved in a committee, but your colleague may have seen your post on LinkedIn. No-one is going to post your achievements, contributions and endeavours for you. But doing this will allow you to stay visible even with those you don't engage with daily.

7. If you get positive feedback from your team members or project stakeholders, ensure that you circulate this to your management team. If a subcontractor has noted that you are great to work with during tendering, you can forward this onto your manager with a note – *Thank you for giving me the opportunity to work on this tender, it's allowed me to build great relationships to get pricing in future.* The note isn't about you directly, but about the business, yet at the same time it's highlighting your effort.

Self-promotion doesn't need to feel 'icky', as most people frequently note that's what it feels like. If your goals and progression are not more important than you leaving your comfort zone, then you don't deserve your goals. The benefit you can yield from achieving your goals, having access to opportunities, being able to have leverage in negotiations, boosting your future opportunities and professional reputation outweigh the cost of you temporarily feeling uncomfortable. A business is always self-promoting, so if you want to succeed, start thinking and acting like a business too.

'Visibility is not vulnerability. It is an important step on the ladder of success to stand out as an individual.' – Daphne Michaels

TRIGGER QUESTIONS

1. What would it mean to your career opportunities if more people in the industry knew who you were?
2. Imagine if you could access off-market opportunities because more influential people in the industry knew who you were. What benefit would this yield your progress, remuneration and recognition?
3. Do you plan to do your best work in the dark and use hope as a strategy that opportunity will come to you?
4. Do you have limiting beliefs when it comes to self-promotion? What is the cost of these beliefs?
5. If you won't promote yourself, who will?
6. How are you going to overcome the fear of putting yourself out there online?

YOUNG GUN BULLETS

- Post valuable content on social media reflective of your personal and professional lives at least once a week. Without content and social media engagement, how will people know you exist in their online networks? Other than social media, are there online blogs that you can contribute a piece to?
- Identify any industry awards that you can nominate yourself for. There are associations that run annual awards and being recognised on such a platform will hugely boost your visibility and credibility.

- Once you have found an association that aligns with your values from N (N – Networking), other than seeking to get on a committee, look to see how you can contribute in terms of speaking or being a panellist to share your industry experiences.

W

WORTHINESS

WÛR'THĒ- NĒSS

THE QUALITY OF BEING WORTHY; HONOUR;

EXCELLENCE; DIGNITY; VIRTUE; MERIT

'Stand up for yourself by not standing yourself up.'
– Gina Greenlee

You were born worthy. Everything you desire is already yours. Except no-one owes you anything in the pursuit of achieving your goals and ambitions. You are not entitled to anything. Anything you desire is only going to come from the direction of your own consistent thoughts and actions towards it. There is no-one who will wake up in the morning and think, *I will do everything I can in my power, all day and everyday to ensure that [name] is a standout success.* The only person who should be awaking with that thought is you. What are your actual expectations in the pursuit of success? Whether it's your career, business, body, mind or soul, who's going to do the inner and outer work for you? There are some people who have such a deep sense of entitlement that they openly demand people who are successful to do everything they can and solve all their problems and realise all their dreams for them whilst they literally sit back and do nothing. It's abhorrent that people in today's age, where there is no shortage of anything other than resourcefulness, display entitlement. The rules of any game are simple – you must earn the prizes, not demand them. If you desire success, you need to become worthy of success. Who do you have to become to be the person who has the success you dream of? Imagine yourself wanting to work for the greatest entrepreneur of all time. Who do you have to be to get their attention? To be worthy of their attention? Are they interested in those who are lax in life with no conviction? Or would they rather have the hungry, consistent and ambitious on their team? If success was a person, would they want to spend time with you? What are the compelling reasons you would give success to hang around you?

YOUNG GUN PRINCIPLE

Ayoung gun expects nothing from anyone and no guarantees or promises along their journey to success, yet continues with belief, diligence and fervour all the same without waning in effort.

Now let's look at it in the context that you are likely to find yourself in, and that is discussions around pay and promotion at work. I interview many executives and CEOs who share similar frustrations when it comes to entitlement, especially in the workplace. From their perspective from most people, they hear, 'I want, I want and I want.' The employee mindset is the one which is focused on their own comforts and what they can get from someone else. If a CEO has hundreds of staff working for them, come pay and promotion time, how many demands and ultimatums do you think they face? This needs to be flipped. The only way to get all you want is to enable others to get what they want. You add value to yourself after adding value to others first. Simply demanding what you desire from your workplace doesn't make you worthy of it. Why does an employer have to provide this? The onus is on you to demonstrate your value and worthiness to have what you desire from the workplace. Most do the absolute minimum and expect the absolute maximum. Everyone is in sales, and it's your own job to demonstrate your value, so as to be worthy of receiving additional benefits from your workplace. The days are over where you can rely on tenure or meeting role requirements to do that. If you desire more pay than what the company is offering, you need to demonstrate how you will also deliver more value than they're expecting and how this will benefit the company. Will it be a worthwhile investment for them to pay you what you're asking? The same is for promotions. It's on you to present the business case as to why it would be a great idea for the company to promote you. This is where most people falter when it comes to pay and promotion within the workplace as they make it a sheer expectation based on tenure. The responsibility of learning the persuasion, influence, communication, psychology and negotiation to get what you want in the workplace needs to happen outside of the workplace.

Instead of investing twelve months to learn and capitalise on this for the rest of their life, most people will be entitled and simply expect the organisation to provide on a never-ending basis. You're not simply owed anything by being an employee, it needs to be earnt. There are no shortages of employees, the professional marketplace has an oversupply, so if you desire to keep a position, earn it.

YOUNG GUN PRINCIPLE

First you become, then you achieve. The onus is on you to become the person who has massive, holistic success. The onus to develop and represent this is also on you.

Prior to any pay or promotion meeting, the metrics of role success need to be clearly defined. When the goalposts are vague, so are the ways to prove that they've been met. Cal Newport, author of *Deep Work,* calls the concept of having unclear metrics that define your success in a position as a 'metric black hole'. Without the metrics, knowing whether you're doing a great job or not becomes a subjective exercise. It's different for a physical labourer, who can quite frankly measure how many metres of defect-free concrete has been laid. However, for 'knowledge workers' this isn't as clear. Newport quotes, 'In the absence of clear indicators of what it means to be productive and valuable in their jobs, many knowledge workers turn back toward an industrial indicator of productivity: doing lots of stuff in a visible manner.' This is where people base their value on basic metrics such as attendance, going to all meetings – in other words, basic role requirements. Simply being present at work and looking busy, or even being there the longest, is a vanity metric. Make sure that there is a clear and objective assessment of performance, and that you have a copy of it to work towards and surpass.

Once the goalposts have been set, consider if the type of value and worth you want to demonstrate is intensive value or extensive value. This is a concept by Robert Greene, author of *The 48 Laws of Power*. In his book, he describes intensive value to be generated from mastery of a specific skill that you've developed over time. You could be a master programmer or the best with financials on the project. You could be the person who knows every single process and form within the business, making you the go-to person. Extensive value is when you are the connector, meaning your value is derived from your relationships with others. You are the individual that connects and collects the right people and information to get tasks done. Without you, no-one would necessarily know how to keep things moving. Long-term value demonstration exists in either sphere and not in the middle mediocre band. To develop intensive value, you want to gain as much knowledge and insight on the skill as possible. For example, the marketing lead would want to know all there is about marketing and human psychology. They would seek to be in constant engagement with the latest in the field. To develop extensive value, you would be spending most time on relationship equity, understanding how the macro environment operates, knowing the people and what they're really good at, and who needs what in a project or a team so you can make it happen. You will find that people who gravitate towards extensive value become organisational leaders, and intensive value orientated people become great managers or specific team leads. Both are valuable, but you need to consider where your speciality lies so you can work towards being a person of such great value that they'll never want to let you go.

Here are five tactical time-tested ways to demonstrate your value and worth come pay and promotion time:

1. Be sure to demonstrate the benefit of your work, not just the features. Don't just tell someone what you did but how it benefitted their objectives. You can't assume that this is a given. Engaging in healthy eating and exercising regularly is also a given, but how much marketing needs to be pumped into this message to get people to do it? Most people don't immediately see the benefit of anything, the onus is on you to sell it.

2. Highlight not just what you did for yourself, but also for your team. When the organisation prospers, you also prosper. For the organisation to prosper, your team members must be as optimised as you are. Keep a record of how you have also enabled your team members to achieve outcomes, as this demonstrates your ability to truly be a key part of the overall organisational growth.

3. Ask your manager for input into your development plan to achieve your goals inside the organisation. Don't just sit around waiting for them to come to you and identify what your goals are. You need to tell them, and then be proactive about getting their input on the plan to achieve it. When you get buy-in from decision-makers early on about your progression, you have a clear path with less ambiguity to get there. For example, if your goal is to get a $15,000 pay

rise, which may be above average in your role, you would ask your lead what they would expect from you in order to grant this. This is a stronger approach than simply expecting a payrise because the year has elapsed. When you tie in your goals based on company goals, the company can see value in you as an asset.

4. In the same merit, don't ask for a payrise on all the work that you have already completed. When you are seeking a pay increase, you need to highlight your future value based on past performance as evidence. Most people request more money for work they have already been remunerated for.

5. Use value-related words in your discourse, such as achieved, created, increased, generated, improved, launched, saved, under budget. These are words that show how value was created in specific scenarios. Using precise language to high-light the achievements is key to making it memorable and distinct.

Remember that businesses pay for value, not just your time. In consideration that an average career is approximately ninety thousand hours, why stay in the middle, grey band of mediocrity instead of maximising your value proposition? In the word extraordinary, you will find the word extra. To have what others won't have, and to be what others won't be, you must do what others won't. This is extra. Long gone are the days of going to and from work to alone get you all you want to achieve. You are in the business of sales, and the more that you can market and sell your value and worth, the more that you will attract success.

'When you start seeing your worth, you'll find it harder to stay around people who don't.' – Anonymous

TRIGGER QUESTIONS

1. Do you believe you are worthy of everything you desire?
2. If you don't see your worth, how do you expect others to?
3. When did you decide that you are not worthy or lesser than those around you? Are those beliefs serving you or hindering you?
4. Do you feel confident in selling your value without diminishing your value?
5. What do you value the most about yourself and your abilities? What makes you the proudest of you?
6. What is one thing you wished other people noticed more about you? How can you integrate this quality in action and conversation daily?

YOUNG GUN BULLETS

- Be conscious of the language used when detailing your value. When talking about your value and achievements, use 'I' not 'we'. This makes your direct contribution clear without hiding behind a team. What also diminishes your value is the constant use of 'sorry'. Someone knocks into you, why do you apologise? You mixed up some papers on the printer, why apologise? The overuse of sorry makes one appear weaker and subservient. Use it sparingly and only when a real apology is in order.

- Set up a meeting in the first quarter of the year to discuss your developmental plan and goals with your manager. This needs to be done before formal pay and performance reviews, so you know the exact KPIs that you need to meet in order to achieve your career outcomes come pay and performance review time.

- Actively seek a coaching or mentoring program that will enable you to learn high-income skills that you wouldn't necessarily have exposure to in the foundational years of your career. Relying on your employment to provide you with all the development you need is a mediocre approach and one that leaves opportunity on the table. The onus has always been on you, and there's no compelling reason to wait for your employer to show you the road.

X

XENODOCHIAL

ZɛNə'DOƱKIəL

FRIENDLY TO STRANGERS

'A friend to all is a friend to none.' – Aristotle

If anything, after reading this section, you would have learnt a new word. The construction industry is a people industry after all, and you will be coming across strangers on the daily. The ability to connect with any person from any pathway will always serve you well. Some people's natural demeanour may be authoritative and direct, but that isn't the antithesis of being friendly, they're just direct. This isn't to suggest you need to be phoney or an over-the-top friendly person to display this attribute. The most subtle way to demonstrate this is by simply talking to people and expressing curiosity to getting to know a stranger. And if smiling is natural to you, then smile, it's an inviting facial expression upon meeting someone. Being friendly is more about having an aura that is inviting, and not about being everyone's friend.

There is a difference between being liked and being respected. Someone can respect you based on your achievements and results, but they may not like you. To be able to extend respect to someone else because of what they have done and not like them, is also a marker of maturity. However, displaying likeability can certainly only benefit you, not hinder you, as you progress. The aim is always to be respected, not liked. If you want to be liked, go and sell icecream and be everything to everyone, which is impossible. I used to be hung up on whether people liked me or not, then I realised how impossible that would be to achieve without losing my sense of self and becoming a people-pleaser. You don't have to be friends with your colleagues and want to spend time with them outside of work hours. Forty to fifty hours with the same people can be more than enough at times, but this also doesn't mean that you're unfriendly. To display a level of amicability in the workplace, take initiative in conversation. If someone is sharing something from their personal life then that can be a cue for you to share equal amounts, but not greater. I never discuss my personal life without an invitation to do so. Eventually with enough insights into you, your colleagues can perceive you as amicable. Coming across as amicable is also aided by giving genuine praise and being complementary, but only when it is genuine. Remember, the goal is to attain respect, not likeability.

> # YOUNG GUN PRINCIPLE
> Approach those you don't know with no biases and a
> genuine curiosity to get to know the other person.

Wherever you go, you will continuously come across people from a diverse range of backgrounds and customs. In addition to emotional intelligence, there is a growing demand for social intelligence. Social intelligence is having the foresight and insight to understand that what may seem normal and natural for you to do, may come across as offensive to another culture or vice versa. First, never stereotype and assume that one person is a representation of a whole culture. For example, don't assume that someone who is of Asian descent is great at math. If you make such a comment, it makes you sound ignorant. Second, never mark their ways or what they deem as norm as weird. It can make someone feel uncomfortable. For example, if someone is eating lunch and it's not your meat pie, don't tell them it looks or smells strange. And yes, I've seen this happen from people who haven't yet connected their brain to their mouth. It is precisely the differences between us that makes life and getting to know others interesting. Only through conversation and curiosity will you start to pick up on their nuances which will allow you to interact and connect with others with more impact. Through my collaboration partnership, I do mentoring and coaching work in India. There are certain phrases and terms that make sense here, but over there gets lost in translation. It's my duty to learn their customs, business language and nuances of interaction to develop my cultural intelligence. It's not just about being friendly to strangers but understanding them and valuing their differences.

Acknowledging diversities as such allows you to speak someone else's language and foster grounds for connection.

'Charisma is the intangible that makes people want to follow you, to be around you, to be influenced by you.' – Roger Dawson

Have you come across people who just seem to have this magnetic pull to them? They just seem so charming. It's charisma. People want to be in the presence of people with charisma. They are those people when you go to an event that you want to be in the company of. It's hard to put your finger on what makes them magnetic, but they are. They have this natural air of cool, calm and collected confidence. Not everyone has the same amount of charisma, and arguably, some just don't have it at all no matter what they do. However, considering that charisma is the ability to relate, attract and influence people, be accepted by others as someone who is interesting and a pleasant individual to be around, this can be generated by you too. Charisma is rooted in values and feelings. It's influence of the combination that Aristotle called the *logos,* the *ethos* and the *pathos.* This means to persuade others, you must use powerful and reasoned rhetoric, proven personal and moral credibility, and then deeply rouse and connect with the emotions of those around you. According to a Harvard study, eight of the past ten US presidents who deployed tactical charismatic traits, won. There has been further accredited large-scale studies that have shown charisma to be an invaluable asset in any work context, in any culture or size of organisation. *The Harvard Review* found that charismatic people are excellent orators that use the power of metaphors, similes and analogies to connect and convey a message. Storytelling is a powerful and memorable vehicle to truly move people and allows people to relate what you are saying to something they are already familiar with. Plus, via storytelling is how people remain hooked into your presence – they want to hear the story. Charismatic people are also expressive people, having bold expressions of moral conviction and passions. When you are the person in conversation who is expressing the collective values, goals and aspirations of your people, they'll be drawn to you and even in awe of you. Sincerity is a critical factor in building charisma, as people can sense when someone is being inauthentic or putting on a show.

YOUNG GUN PRINCIPLE

You can only be all of who you are if you know who you are. Being genuine is more important to you and everyone around you than being friendly.

Which leads me to one of the key insights that will change all your interactions with others. That is being genuine and authentic. Most people will see right through someone who is being ingenuine, even if they can't put their finger on why, but they get the feeling from their aura. Most people don't know who they are because they don't take any time to identify their person. How much time do you invest getting to know yourself on the macro and micro? Would you be able to describe your person without describing your degree, experience, job title or work history in sixty seconds? If the answer is no, you don't know yourself. You've been spending too much time looking outwards than inwards. When you are genuine, you are consistent in how you do everything instead of being a chameleon given the scenario. Being genuine is being all of who you are, but you can't do that if you don't know who you are. It requires you to believe what you are saying to other people, and being genuine in conversation always takes precedence over being friendly to them. When someone is inauthentic, trust is broken. Whereas when someone is authentic, they have this natural gravitas to them. People are inherently attracted to uniqueness and individuality. Those that are inauthentic may also try too hard to impress and generate likeability, whereas genuine people don't try to make people like them. It takes extremely thick skin to be genuine and to stand strong in your sense of self in this current society, but it is the guaranteed path to standing out in a credible and notable way in a sea of sameness and people who are fragments of themselves. As American novelist Nathaniel Hawthorne said, 'No one man can, for any considerable time, wear one face to himself and another to the multitude, without finally getting bewildered as to which is the true one.'

TRIGGER QUESTIONS

1. Are you quick to jump to conclusions when you meet new people?
2. Do you have a genuine curiosity to get to know people when you meet them?
3. How do you know if you are harbouring biases towards groups of people? Have you examined your belief system?

4. Are you open and honest in conversation, or do you only tell people what they want to hear?

5. Can you talk about yourself sans your experiences, titles and degrees? Write out your response to 'tell me about yourself'. Review your first answer – does it fully encompass your person? Does it talk about your passions or just your work to-do list?

6. Think about conversations you've had that have truly moved you and connected with you. What was it about those conversations that elicited a strong emotional connection? Why was this conversation more memorable than the average work ones that you have?

YOUNG GUN BULLETS

- Make a conscious effort to speak to someone new every day for five to ten minutes. This could be onsite, in your office or even the local barista. What can you learn about a new person daily? This will increase your bandwidth of conversation, but in comparison to people who are always disengaged, on their phone or rushing, your genuine interest will be a welcomed change.

- Dale Carnegie famously said, 'A person's name is the sweetest sound in the world to that person.' When you are in conversation, say people's names. It will immediately catch their attention and make you appear more likeable and present.

- Find common ground as soon as you can in conversation. This is the surest way to build rapport. Venture away from typical work conversations and lead into the personal. By focusing on what's important to others and tying that back to you, you'll start fostering that connection early on. To do this, you need to lavishly ask questions and have a genuine interest to the response.

Y

YEARNING

YÛR'NĬNG

A PERSISTENT, OFTEN MELANCHOLY DESIRE; A

LONGING; STRONG DESIRE

_____

'There are three ingredients to a good life: learning,
earning and yearning.' – Christopher Morley

There are a few characteristics noted until now which cannot be taught to individuals, such as ambition. Either someone has it, or they simply satisfice their way through life being content with the average. Wanting more from life is generally another of those characteristics. I'm a maximalist, not a minimalist. Some will only have a wake-up call to the brevity of our human experience after a terminal illness or a painful event to themselves or someone close to them. Then they may start maximising their time here, rather than minimising it. Why wait for such an event? And why don't you want more from your career and life? Don't you have an insatiable yearning to maximise every aspect of your life? Your career, health, wealth, relationships, spirituality, community, philanthropy, business – the whole lot of it. Yearning is a deep, innate desire of knowing that where you are right now is not all there is. All that you know right now has only gotten you to where are you today. It cannot take you further. Except most people think they already know it all when all they really have is the illusion of knowledge and a lack of self-awareness over their own blind spots. Rest assured that there is more in the sphere of what you don't know that you don't know, than there is in the sphere of what you do know. The minute you stop engaging in learning in the form of personal and professional development is the day that you start going backwards. This is over and above the technical requirements of your work, which doesn't unlock your potential.

YOUNG GUN PRINCIPLE

Have a strong, burning desire for your career and life.
The key to your progress is to be unsatisfied with the
present situation and have a burning desire for your
future outcomes.

Yearning is about never being truly satisfied and having a burning desire to be in the constant pursuit of growth. Having a burning desire is the first principle in *Think and Grow Rich* by Napoleon Hill, one of the greatest personal development books of all time. You can only materialise and achieve that which you have a burning desire for, and that means yearning for it so much with all your mind, body and soul. 'Desire is the starting point of all achievement, not a hope, not a wish, but a keen pulsating desire which transcends everything,' says Napoleon Hill. You will start to observe that many simply have a lukewarm desire, or one that goes cold quick. Or their desire will be like a firebomb, hot at first yet only to settle as quickly as it came about. Whatever it is you desire, lean into it with all you have, consistently. Repeated engagement with the positive thoughts and emotions around what you want is the basis of achievement. So, turn up the temperature on your desires and let them burn.

Second to yearning is curiosity. I somehow am constantly re-amazed at the lack of curiosity that people carry with them. We live in an age where we have access to the entirety of human history and thoughts through a few keyboard functions. There is no excuse for being wilfully ignorant in today's day and age. Even when new learning opportunities, experiences and ideas are put in front of people, they let their fear and certainty run their mind, and thus life, instead of engaging in possibility. Those who don't display curiosity are self-absorbed with their condition and their condition alone, and not with anything that doesn't impact them. Who in your life is constantly asking questions and challenging everything? Why are we taking everything at face value? Before you accept any belief, have you tested it? Why do you have the opinions that you do? We aren't born with our opinions, so where'd they generate from? Why were you put on this planet? Why do most people hate their job? Why do few truly understand the subconscious powerhouse of their mind? Why do people know their job role better than their own person? I could write questions to fill a whole other alphabet, but you get the idea. 'The best in business have boundless curiosity and open minds,' says author Robin Sharma. Not just business, but life itself. For curiosity is an essential ingredient to creativity. You cannot truly unlock your own potential without tapping into the creative faculty of your mind. Have a deep yearning to seek new experiences, ideas and challenges so you can truly learn and grow. Yearning is about seeking – like being an explorer. Add fuel to your curiosity to start engaging in more critical thoughts and become awake to what it truly means to have a human experience. It's more than what you've been told to date, I assure you of this. Simply do not be satisfied so easily and avoid any form of discovery.

'The public have an insatiable curiosity to know everything except what is worth knowing.' – Oscar Wilde

When you yearn, you stay hungry. 'A lion runs the fastest when he is hungry,' said Salman Khan, Indian producer and actor. If you are satisfied, and not hungry, you're not going to be enticed to go get food. You wait until you are hungry again before you take any action. By the time you are resting in-between your rhetorical feed, there is someone out there who is still hunting. Yearning keeps you hungry. You don't have time in the pursuit of your ambition to listen to the naysayers who tell you to 'take it easy' or 'relax'. Let them relax and take it easy and tell them that you'll compare notes with them in ten years' time to see who had the right philosophy on achievement. If I listened to anyone other than those with a vested interest in my success, there wouldn't be one book, let alone three. Even those with a burning ambition to get into the industry and do all these incredible things have their flame extinguished once they get into a job. A job serves as a temporary soothing cream to the pain of standing at the outset of the industry, but eventually that too wears off. Your career and life will take off into levels of success you didn't even know existed if you stay hungry for decades. That alone is a feat, as most people can't sustain any emotion other than fear for extended periods of time.

'Become so curious and obsessed with one thing that you forget everything else. Follow it, drink it, dive deep in it, master it. Remarkable results need remarkable actions.'
— Maxime Lagacé

TRIGGER QUESTIONS

1. How often do you question everything around you? Are you more likely to say, 'It is what it is,' or, 'Why is it like this?'? Do you think you'll have deeper understanding if you seek to be curious instead of wilfully ignorant?
2. How do you handle different perspectives?
3. Are you quick to reject new ideas and alternative viewpoints, or are you curious to discover another perspective?
4. Have you had a long-standing interest in a field outside your chosen career? What are you doing to fuel that interest?
5. Do you have a burning desire to learn and explore or a luke-warm desire? Are you content at constructing your career from just a technical standpoint?

6. What would you want your life's work to look like and encompass? What is the legacy you want to leave behind? Do you want to leave a legacy?

YOUNG GUN BULLETS

- Generate a new experience for yourself every month. If you assess the diversity of experiences of an average professional, you'll see they have the repeat button stuck in a continuous loop. This could be in any area of interest to you. Especially as a young gun, you aren't in a position to say no to new experiences. There's so much that you truly have no idea about, so why limit yourself?

- Do you have an entrepreneurial itch? Start a side hustle or find additional ways to add streams of income. Do you find yourself buying a product or a service saying you can do it better? Well, here's your chance. What you learn in the world of business in one year is worth over ten in corporate alone. Second to exploring your spirituality, understanding business and entrepreneurship will offer you the most personal and professional expansion. Your career isn't a one-dimensional piece of construction, and you should be building multiple career pathways that reflect your multidimensional interests and talents. One size career certainly does not fit all.

- Get into the habit of recording your thoughts and ideas. Collect them. Letting your mind wander is imperative to following your curiosities. However, sometimes we have a great idea that becomes a fleeting thought, and we say we'll come back to it later only to not remember it. Whether it's a notebook that's always by your side or a notes application, fill it with quotes and ideas that spark your curiosity.

Z

ZEALOUS

ZĔL'əS

FILLED WITH OR MOTIVATED BY ZEAL; FERVENT

'To escape the curse of commoditisation, a company has to be a gamechanger, and that requires employees who are proactive, inventive and zealous.' – Gary Hamel

Derived from the Greek work *zelos*, to be zealous means to have an 'ardour or fervour of spirit'. There is an energy and an enthusiasm about one in all they do. They're all-in, on fire, they are pure energy. You can feel their presence, they're expressive and they truly have a thirst and hunger for life. They approach everything they're passionate about with equal enthusiasm. Does this sound like a person you'd love to be around? Except most people are energy vampires. There's no zeal. When you ask some people how they are, they can barely muster up the energy to give a flatlined 'good' in response. Everything in this lifetime is energy, and when you assess people's energy over the long run, they are as flat as a pancake. The suppression of your energy is the suppression of what it means to have a human experience. Why is this important? First, if you continuously dull yourself down on an energetic plane to fit in, then that's all you have achieved being – another face in an unenergetic crowd. Second, you cannot attract anything from a reduced level of energy. What massive opportunity will come to you if your energy is of a low vibration? Nothing worth having. I understand this is unconventional to be mentioning when it comes to a book for construction, but that's precisely the issue. The factor that impacts your success the most and has the most influence is the least spoken about. It is my duty to bring it into your conscious awareness, so you can truly focus on the arenas that will bring you the greatest progress. I would encourage you to look into the work of Nikola Tesla on electromagnetic body field auras, so you can start to realise that we are first energetic beings before physical beings. The more energetic you are, the more people will be drawn to you. By mere fact of being more energetic, you will stand out from a flatlined team. Being zealous reflects having an energetic desire to see something succeed, not just an intellectual desire. There is a world of different between the two, with one making you a magnet for success and the other leaving people wondering why many don't have the success they wish to see for themselves.

Especially when it comes to the workplace, energy management is key. Construction is a high-stress environment, with lots on the line. Millions of dollars riding on projects, the safety of people, meeting client demands. Construction sites, especially those that aren't well managed, are pressure pots. It can be demanding to get swept up in the fervent emotions and stresses of site. Doing this continuously over time leaves people depleted. Consider a person running a marathon. They exert their energy in a balanced, sustainable way so they can be in it for the long haul. Those who leave the mark with a burst of energy find themselves left with little in the tank to get to the finish line. It's no different to working in construction. Knowing when to react and expend energy or emotion (note that emotion simply stands for energy in emotion) is key to your long-term, sustained success. When situations onsite aren't going your way or it's a stressful time on the project, control your energy. You want to be a bottle of water when you are shaken or stirred. A bottle of water doesn't erupt when outside conditions are turbulent. A bottle of soda, however, will certainly erupt when it is shaken and has pressure applied. I truly learnt energy management in the last two years of my corporate career. I needed a significant amount of energy in the evenings to serve clients, work on my business and in my business, and it wasn't beneficial to be depleted by the end of the day. So, I approached situations with a more balanced approach and learnt how to conserve my energy. I was able to not get swept up in unnecessary emotions and expend unnecessary energy for no return. This isn't to say you don't show that you care, but you are controlling your own energetic state. You will find yourself being able to run marathons instead of short 100m sprints.

YOUNG GUN PRINCIPLE

Young guns will seek to engage themselves in work that brings them energy instead of depleting them, so they can operate at a high vibration comparatively to their peers.

To be energetic for most of the time would require you to be engaged in your passions. When I get to write my books, I'm energised. When I get to mentor and coach, I'm extremely energised. When I have dynamic podcast recordings with value-aligned guests, it's energising. And what brings pure energy is seeing my clients win. If your own passion and vision doesn't bring you energy, then what will? Society has made it out to be that constructing your career on your passion is fools' play. Certainly, someone who is passionate about ice cream but has no business or culinary skills, shouldn't quit their job tomorrow to open an ice cream shop. When you are passionate about something, there's an inherent level of enthusiasm, because it's what lights up the heart, mind and soul and it's all you want to be filling up your time with. When you follow your passion, success will start to flow to you because you're working in total alignment with what you should be doing not what you've been told to do. When people are of low energy and enthusiasm, it leaves them feeling lost, confused and stuck, which is the consequence of being disengaged from your passion. As said by Oprah Winfrey, 'Forget about the fast lane. If you really want to fly, harness your power to your passion. Honour your calling. Everybody has one. Trust your heart, and success will come to you.' If you're not following your passion, you're working against

209

your natural grain and disposition. Have the heart and courage to follow what it is you are being called to, so as to approach life with a deep-founded zeal.

The journey of finding your passion is one of the most valuable you will go on. There are some who say that they don't have a passion. You do, it just hasn't been found. In the interim, approach everything you do with passion and energy. The following are practical ways in which you can increase your energy on a day-to-day basis until you get to the point where the zealousness is eternally lit from within naturally. Whilst the mechanisms to control your energy from a mind, body and soul perspective are extensive, I have only listed those that right now offer no barriers to implementation or heavy lifting to get immediate results:

1. Incorporate more movement and exercise in your day. Office people are quite sedentary beings, which not only has compounding physical disadvantages but also energetic ones. Exercising leads to higher dopamine levels which works to increase your mood. Identify pockets in your day to regularly exercise and get more movement. For example, if you must walk to a meeting, walk faster.

2. Be conscious of what you are feeding your body. Remember, you live in your mind and body, so look after it. You may be stressed and time-poor, which is where fast food may become the easy option. And if you work on sites, those easy-access food trucks don't help. Eat to increase your energy. The construction culture is one addicted to caffeine. It continuously surprises people on sites that I don't drink coffee. Coffee does increase alertness but an over-reliance on it will leave you

dealing with too many slumps during the day. Use water to combat fatigue instead of caffeine.

3. Limit or distance your interactions with negative people. There is always someone in the office who has a bleak and devastating outlook on everything. They are always complaining about anything they can. If you find yourself in conversation with an individual that leaves your energy depleted, learn to distance them as much as you can. The negativity of others can be an energy blackhole if you aren't careful. Learn how to surround yourself with other zealous people.

4. Feed your mind in the morning with affirmations, positive self-talk and visualise how you want to run the day, instead of letting the day run you. Priming your mind allows you to prepare yourself for the day. It's even more effective to say these affirmations out loud. Most people, when they wake up, engage in a freight train of negative thoughts and consume their mind with tasks and demands at work. There are truly only two things in this world that you can control: your thoughts and your emotions. If you cannot control these, then you cannot control anything else. This priming needs to be done in the morning before you start your day to get optimal long-term results.

5. Sit in silence and breathe deeply. There can be situations at work or onsite which are truly hair-raising and frustrating. Never react straight away but take a few minutes of silence and breathe deeply to level out the emotion.

6. Listen to music, podcasts or other content that is empowering and inspirational. When you flood your mind with

positivity and content that supports your goals and ambitions, you are more likely to shift your own outlook. You will operate less from a modality of fear and more from a modality of possibility. You need to be conscious about what you are consuming from a content perspective, so find content that serves you. If your social media leaves you feeling insecure instead of energised, unfollow who you need to and find more aligned content.

If a negative event has occurred during the day, learn to be mindful and not let your reaction seep into every crevasse of your life. You cannot change the fact that an event happened, but you can control your reaction to it. One of my favourite projects was extremely under pressure from every direction possible. One Saturday evening a hot water pipe burst on level four. By the time the leak was discovered early Monday morning, significant damage had been done. The project manager was extremely level and focused on steering the ship. I was extremely impressed at how he maintained a balanced disposition. He left at 5pm like he always did and left the work issues at work. A reactive young gun cannot effectively serve the team whatever happens, so learn to control your emotional responses.

> 'One person with a divine purpose, passion and power is better than ninety-nine people who are merely interested. Passion is stronger than interest.' – Israelmore Ayivor

One zealous person who is committed and enthusiastic is bound to attract more opportunities than one who is merely interested in their work. Bring more zeal into your interactions and watch how those around you also start to respond to you. Zealous people live a life of expressiveness instead of suppression and have a good balance of being driven from their heart and not just their mind. Being zealous isn't about being the loudest, but it certainly commands attention in a room full of people who are disconnected from their heart and mind. If you seek extraordinary results, you must be on an extraordinary vibration.

TRIGGER QUESTIONS

1. Is there a cause you are truly passionate about?
2. If money wasn't an issue, would you still be working on what you are right now? How would you truly spend your time if you weren't salary dependent?
3. What will you start doing moving forward to instil more energy in your interactions?
4. What beliefs do you have about yourself and your ability to succeed in pursuing your main passion in life?
5. How have your limiting beliefs and fears held you back from finding or pursuing your main passion in the past? What is the main concern that's holding you back from committing to pursuing your primary passion in life?
6. If you don't know your passion yet, how can you instil more passion into what you are doing right now?

YOUNG GUN BULLETS

- Instil ten times more energy into your interactions. Notice how flatline the response is when you ask people how they are. Respond with more energy when asked in return and watch their surprise.
- Become more expressive in your voice and body movements. When you smile, smile with your whole face. Use your hands when you talk. Notice how still most people are, which is a consequence of conformity. Come alive when you interact, instead of being a fragment of yourself.
- Take stock of what depletes you of energy – people, places, projects? Cut out sources of energy deficiencies without hesitation and surround yourself with what does.

CONCLUSION

What makes you think you will be successful?

Are you familiar and well-versed with the time-tested principles and laws of success?

Could you articulate to someone else the precise formulae for achieving whatever it is you want to constantly be a stand-out success?

The answer should be no, and that response should be the trigger to realise your success education to be all that you can has only just begun. Once you truly have a deep inner-standing of what it really takes to achieve success and be a stand-out in this world, you will never see the world the same. It would become expansive instead of suppressive because you will realise that it all starts and ends with you, and how much opportunity there is for those with real ambition and a fire in their heart. I know, as I've been down that road of truly doing the deep inner work required and now have the fortunate ability to coach and mentor on the same. It's a fool's game to think that you already know all that you need to know, or that success will come through sheer talent, virtue or goodwill.

If you were seeking a technical handbook for construction

success, then you haven't come to the right place. I wanted to ensure that each section gave you deep insight to learn what isn't spoken about in corporate, and to allow you to bypass the time it takes to even get exposure to this. If you don't know the rules of the game, you can't win the game. Everyone is playing some game. People don't get to great heights in their career by sheer chance or virtue. They know the rules and what levers to push and pull to get the intended outcomes they desire. Be the exception, not the conventional rule. And the key rule you need to know is that other than playing within moral and ethical considerations, there are no rules. It's a free game for all.

If you have read this far, I do commend you. Most people will read the table of contents and think that mere exposure to the chapter titles has impressed on them the entirety of the book. Now that you have read the book, my question to you is who do you want to be? What person do you want to become in the industry? Are you going to be a young gun? This book is about the person you need to become and demonstrate to step into to achieve what you want. It's about your performance, direction, quality of thoughts, habits, paradigms and beliefs, and this has nothing to do with your degree, organisation and certainly not your job title. A young gun is the composite of the former, not the latter. Take away all externalities, it comes down to the standard you wish to hold yourself to in the pursuit of unravelling your own potential.

As someone with great ambition and vision, you may arrive at a point in your corporate career where it doesn't feel sufficient anymore. You can still be a young gun but on your own terms. Looking to succeed in multiple career paths parallel to your seven to five is more than encouraged, for the skills, exposure and experience you will garner. There may even come the turning point to turn to a type of entrepreneurship to create the life and lifestyle you desire. Never fit your dreams to suit the current mode of reality but change the mode of reality to suit your dreams.

There is one trait that is key and aspired to by just about all young guns, and that is confidence. I haven't made confidence its own section, because as you work to implement 100% of the learnings in this book, will you have built up your confidence. You already have confidence but have chosen not to acknowledge it. Confidence also comes after the doing, and through momentum and action. You don't generate more confidence for yourself by remaining static and locked into inaction. However, to get confidence, and to truly step into what it means to be a young gun, takes courage. Where do you see courage being represented in the people around you? When was the last time you demonstrated courage? Most people aren't courageous, they are glued to their comfort zone. Without courage, nothing can eventuate in your life. Think about it. It takes courage to raise your hand in a meeting, courage to stand up for what you believe in. Everything worth having and experiencing starts with courage. To be a young gun, is to have a courageous heart and mind.

Which now begs the question, what are you going to do? Are you going to put this book on your shelf, allowing it to be another shelf-help book? That's what many will do and go back into their work doing what they've been doing before and expect a different outcome. However, there has never been a greater time to be a young gun, if you choose to take the path less travelled. The choice is yours.

Connect with me on social media (Elinor Moshe on LinkedIn

and @elinormoshe_ on Instagram) and tell me what your grand next step is plus your key takeaways from the book. Because I want to see you win.

You're a young gun – so let's lock and load and show the industry who you really are.

ACKNOWLEDGMENTS

As you're traversing through different experiences and conversations, you don't always know in the moment how it will continue to serve you and define you. All the highs and lows of the lessons impressed upon me from my corporate career have allowed me to encapsulate it in this guide for you. So that you can be the exceptional, exemplary and excellent young gun that the construction industry so desperately needs.

The experience of working in construction is most moulded by the people behind the projects. I do need to thank the great personnel of the industry that I have worked with during my time on project delivery, and those that I've had the honour of being in conversation with, especially on my podcast. There were some real A-teams along the journey. You taught me what excellent looks like and what best practice is. But in equal measure, I must thank the inadequate and low-competence people I have worked with. For you also taught me what subpar looks like and exactly what not to do. In retrospect, I would still go through both experiences because it allowed me to arrive exactly where I am today, and that, I wouldn't change.

This book for me personally was a cathartic experience, to

cement and close the years in corporate as I leave it behind permanently as I follow my entrepreneurial pursuits, and above all, my own vision and ambition. The final years of my corporate career were suffocating for me, to say the least. When you're establishing yourself, it takes time to make the transition, but there wasn't a day that went by since I conceived my vision that I didn't dream of the days that I experience today. I learnt to convert the sh*t of my final corporate years into fuel to stay hungry and in every waking hour I had around that go towards my own vision. And I did, and it paid off. Corporate didn't change, I changed, and I wouldn't change the experience for anything. If everything was smooth sailing in corporate, I may not have been instigated to conceive my own vision. I'm glad I hit major turbulence, it made me stop and look out the window to see what was really going on. And I had to go through those experiences to be able to write this book and be able to identify excellence by experiencing the opposite. I'm grateful for the corporate journey, as it provided the sound foundation and runway to do what I so uniquely do today, but I'm even more grateful that we're no longer a fit for each other.

Thank you to my mentors, Ron Malhotra and Caroline Vass, for showing me the pathway to never quell my ambition and for giving me the ability to be more, do more and have more. I have achieved more with you in two years than the entirety of all the years combined prior to meeting you. You've given me the courage at every step of the way and always brought the fuel to my fire. I'm truly proud of the young gun I am today because of each conversation had with you both, and that you allow me to stand on your shoulders of greatness.

I appreciate my parents who have extended their unwavering

support in the pursuit of any ambition that I have chosen to set my mind to. Never underestimate the power of a support network that enables you, not hinders you. They have always provided the strongest foundations for me to launch from and do anything that I set my mind to.

And a heartfelt thank you to each and every constructor who I've the opportunity to mentor and be part of their journey to success. It's the relationship and conversations with you that served as the original impetus to writing this book by being a witness to your growth. I always want you all to win, and thank you for choosing me as your personal construction coach.

ABOUT THE AUTHOR

Elinor Moshe is an ambitious and driven Thought Leader, best-selling author, podcast host and businesswoman disrupting the construction industry. She's the founder of The Construction Coach; Australia's first construction coach. As the podcast host of *Constructing You*, Elinor interviews exemplary leaders and industry titans who dominate construction business and careers. She is the two-time bestselling author of one-of-a-kind books, *Constructing Your Career* and *Leadership in Construction*. She ties her distinctive thinking, uncommon insights with over eight years' experience in the commercial construction industry, to generate transformative and exceptional results for her clients. Elinor has been featured by *Passion Vista* as a 2021 Woman Leader to Look Up To, *Entrepreneur Asia Pacific* as part of 'Top 5 Business Leaders who are making a genuine impact in 2021', *Yahoo! Finance, Australian National Construction Review* and over forty global podcasts discussing her career, leadership and business acumen. She holds a Master of Construction Management and Bachelor of Environments from the University of Melbourne. Her passion is to construct exceptional futures, and that starts with constructing *you*. Elinor lives in Melbourne, Australia.

www.ingramcontent.com/pod-product-compliance
Lightning Source LLC
Chambersburg PA
CBHW031849200326
41597CB00012B/328